The House Of Fear Presents
DEAD OF NIGHT
DAN BIANCHI

HOUSE OF FEAR PUBLICATIONS
New York City, New York
HouseOfFearNyc@aol.com

To Cynthia

The House Of Fear Presents
DEAD OF NIGHT
By Dan Bianchi
Copyright c. 2012

ISBN-13: 978-1470016807
ISBN-10: 147001680X

BISAC: Drama / Anthologies

DEAD OF NIGHT

All Scripts By Dan Bianchi
Adapted From Stories By Listed Authors

Welcome to the Theatre Of Imagination!

The House Of Fear Presents offers easy-to-read, easy-to-produce scripts to those who want to create a unique style of theatrical presentation...and they make for fine reading, as well! Also, they contain unique content found in the genres of HORROR, WEIRD and SCIENCE FICTION.   However, these specially formatted scripts may also be produced as RECORDED WORKS, RADIO BROADCASTS...or, they may even be used as the basis for FILM and VIDEO presentations.

Though most of these scripts have been created to blend both intimate story-telling and cinematic styles requiring recorded SOUND DESIGN, MUSIC CUES and voices on MICROPHONES ...in which there are no props, no sets, no costumes...some stories may be adapted to fit TRADITIONAL PLAY format.

The House Of Fear Presents stories containing characters, plots and action you won't find in traditional theatre: mad scientists, giant man eating plants, werewolves, vampires, ghosts and intergalactic invasions ....from King Kong smashing Radio City Music Hall and climbing the Empire State Building... to the battlefields of war, or, to the internal voice of a man going insane...from a poignant story of a woman waiting for her husband to die...to a screaming skull frightening the new resident of a haunted house!   Turn the lights down low and turn on your imaginations to fill in the visuals.

Many of the longer stories are classic works of world fiction: THE INVISIBLE MAN, THE WAR OF THE WORLDS, DRACULA, FRANKENSTEIN, THE TIME MACHINE, THE ISLAND OF DR.MOREAU, KING KONG...But, The House Of Fear prides itself on its great collection of famous short works from an earlier time by H.G.Wells, Bram Stoker, H.P.Lovecraft, Edgar Allan Poe, Ambrose Bierce, Robert E.Howard...and, not-so-famous works by long ignored giants of macabre literature, such as, Algernon Blackwood, Edith Nesbit, F.Marion Crawford, Sheridan Le Fanu, etc.

These are tales to be told in near darkness. The scripts require not just great actors, but, great STORY TELLERS.   This role is often listed in a script as NARRATOR.   Sometimes, it may be left to the Director's discretion to cast the NARRATOR as either male or female. The story may also require actors to play multiple characters...or, a Director may choose to cast many actors to play these roles. Minor roles may also be recast as either sex.

All scripts are expertly crafted for presentation by DAN BIANCHI, Artistic Director and Founder of NYC's award-winning, critically acclaimed Radiotheatre. He has worked over 40 years as writer/director in stage and film media, and, to date, he's the most produced, living stage writer in NYC. In most cases, the archaic language of 19th Century works has been updated, but, Mr.Bianchi has tried to retain the literary author's original artistic intention and creation. Characters' names, locations, time frames may be changed. Plots may be condensed, endings may be modified, etc. Remember...the original story was intended to be read as literature and not intended to be presented in a different medium using 21st Century technology. In every case, it is Mr. Bianchi's primary goal to deliver a great story filled with optimal sound design as a most important part of the production.

SOUND DESIGN: Sound effects and dramatic music are an integral part of these stories, as necessary as the actors. Scripts contain some, but, not all, printed sound/music cues necessary to make easier reading. Directors may wish to add or change cues or even provide live music accompaniment. If you do NOT wish to create your own sound design, but, instead wish to purchase pre-recorded cues and music, please contact: houseoffearnyc@aol.com.

For more of The House Of Fear Titles: www.houseoffear.org

All scripts printed under the title THE HOUSE OF FEAR PRESENTS are copyrighted and are protected by copyright laws and conventions.

Copyrights and Royalties
COPYING all or part of a script by any means, including mechanical, photocopying, videotaping, scanning, web posting or other digital media formats without permission is a violation of federal and international copyright law. Please purchase the

correct number of scripts needed for your production. Anyone found in violation of this may be prosecuted to the full extent of the law. In addition, The House of Fear Presents reserves the right to assess an infringement penalty up to ten times the original cost owed for photocopying a script. If you order more than one copy of the same script title, you will be billed and obligated to pay licensing (royalty) fees unless you inform The House Of Fear Presents that your selections are for perusal only.

LICENSING FEES are due when a play is performed in front of any size audience when an admission fee is charged. Class room, free readings and free audience-attended rehearsals are excused. PERFORMANCE RIGHTS will be granted when licensing fees are received by The House Of Fear Presents no later than two weeks prior to the first performance. Violators will be prosecuted to the full extent of the law. An infringement penalty up to ten times the original cost owed will be issued against anyone producing any of the included scripts without first acquiring proper rights.

You may not edit a script without prior permission from the author. No changes, interpolations, or deletions in the text or title shall be made for the purpose of the production. Changing gender of a character or geographic locations are possible as long as it does not change the plot or intent of the author in any way. All requests for changes must be approved in writing by The House Of Fear Presents before a live production. Under no circumstances does making changes to the script exempt one from paying full royalties and properly crediting the author and The House Of Fear Presents.

Whenever a play is produced, due authorship credit must be given on all programs, printing and advertising for the play.

Any material, music or sound effects added to any script enclosed must be in the public domain, or originally produced and owned by the producing company. The House Of Fear Presents will not be held liable for any violation of the above.

Listed licensing fees on the script and on www.houseoffear.org are for live stage productions by AMATEUR groups with maximum seating capabilities below 300. Special arrangements must be made by professional groups and amateur groups with larger seating capacity. Please contact our office for licensing fee quotations: houseoffearnyc@aol.com.   Please include details about the planned performance (seating capacity, price per ticket, etc.) Production rights for any play listed on our website, because of circumstances beyond our control, may be withdrawn at any time without prior notice.

For BROADCAST, FILM and VIDEO rights, please contact: houseoffearnyc@aol.com

THE BLACK CAT
By Dan Bianchi
From A Story By Edgar Allan Poe

Cast - 2m,1w
Length - 20 min.
Synopsis - A man is driven crazy by a cat that haunts him into murder.

(MUSIC)

NARRATOR
(To audience) "I've always been considered a quiet human being. Gentle, even. Since childhood, others have joked that I am too kind hearted. Especially, to animals. I've had a lot of pets. They give me a great deal of joy and comfort. If you're a pet lover, you know what I'm talking about. There is something in the unselfish and self-sacrificing love between a man and a dog, it's hard to describe. It often goes beyond any trust or friendship humans are capable of giving. Well...you can imagine how happy I was to find a wife whose disposition was much like my own. She *knew* I loved pets, so, she didn't mind my menagerie. We had birds, gold-fish, a fine dog, rabbits, a small monkey, and... a cat. The cat...we named him Pluto... was a remarkably large and beautiful animal, entirely black, and clever to an astonishing degree."

(MUSIC ENDS)

WIFE
You know what they say about big black cats? I'm not being superstitious, although, perhaps, we shouldn't ignore what's been said about them, altogether. They're witches, you know? Witches in disguise.

NARRATOR
You can't be serious?

WIFE
I'm just saying...that's all. You treat *Pluto* as your favorite of all your pets. You feed him. He follows you wherever you go...even out into the streets, if you let him.

NARRATOR

You're not jealous, are you?

WIFE

I'm just saying. For years, he's been by your side. Did you ever think, why? No, and *why?* Because you're always inebriated.

NARRATOR

Are you implying…?

WIFE

I'm just saying…you'd better cut out your drinking. You're growing moodier every day. Irritable. You care only about yourself, not about others. And, I don't like that language you've been using lately. And, if you ever…*ever*…raise your hand to me again…or, to your pets? That cat…it gets everything. The rest of the animals…you've neglected. You kicked the dog yesterday.

NARRATOR

I didn't mean to…

WIFE

I'm just saying…the rabbits, the monkey. You get a few drinks in you and you're mean to all of them. Except that damned cat. I'm warning you, you'd better put a stop to all this.

(MUSIC)

NARRATOR

"Eventually, the demon alcohol grew worse upon my temper. Poor Pluto even began to experience its effects. One night, returning home, intoxicated, from the local tavern…"

(CAT HOWL)

What? Well, then, you shouldn't be walking under my feet. What are you looking at? Come here you…you….! *OW!* You bit me! You actually *bit* me! That's what you think of me? Why, I'll…come here! Come here, you little bastard! I'll show you!"

(CAT HOWLING)

"I'm thoroughly disgusted and embarrassed to tell you this, but, I must. I then took from my pocket a pen-knife, opened it, grasped the poor beast by the throat, and deliberately cut out one of its eyes from the socket!

(CAT SCREECHING)

"I know, *I know*...I should be *hanged* for that alone.

(MUSIC)

"The next morning, after I slept off my drunkenness...I realized ...*I saw*...what I had done. I felt...well, how can I describe such a lowly feeling? I was feeble, guilty, remorseful...I don't know. But, then, as the craving came upon me once again...my soul became hardened to what I had done. I just wanted to drink. I found a bottle of wine in the closet and soon drowned all memory of my deed. In the meantime the cat slowly recovered. The socket of the lost eye presented, it is true, a frightful appearance, but he no longer appeared to suffer any pain. He went about the house as usual... but, as might be expected, fled in extreme terror at my approach. At first, I still had a bit of my old feelings left...it hurt me to see him run away whenever I entered a room. Eventually, that feeling grew into irritation. And then, it turned to *anxiety.* That's what liquor will do to you. And *yet,* I continued to drink. I know I shouldn't have, but, I did. The more my wife told me not to, the more I had to. In fact, I began to regard drinking as an act of rebellion by a free spirit. I could do what I want. You can't tell *me* to stop doing it!

(END MUSIC)

"One morning...." *Pluto!* I see you there...staring at me with that one eye of yours. Accusing me, aren't you? Always accusing me. Well, you're not my judge. Come here, you devil! I'll put an end to all this right now!

(MUSIC)

"So, I slipped a noose about its neck and hung it to the limb of a tree. *Why?* Because I knew that it had loved me, and because I felt it had given me *no* reason to harm it. I hung it because *I knew* that, in so doing, I was committing a sin. A deadly sin that would so jeopardize my immortal soul as to place it even beyond the reach of the infinite mercy of the Most

Merciful and *Most Terrible* God. I had rebelled against God. That night...as I lay in my bed sleeping..."

(END MUSIC, FIRE CRACKLING)

WIFE
Fire! Fire!

NARRATOR
"The curtains of my bed were in flames. The whole house was blazing. My wife and I had barely made our escape from the conflagration. The destruction was complete. Our entire worldly wealth was swallowed up."

WIFE
What are we to do now? We've got nothing left...nothing...

(MUSIC)

NARRATOR
"I didn't want to think that what I had done to Pluto might have caused this disaster. The next day, we visited the ruins. The walls had fallen in. Except for one wall which stood about the middle of the house. That's where the head of my bed had been. The plastering there was thick. That's what probably had saved it. But, now...there was my wife examining that wall, pointing to it..."

(END OF MUSIC)

WIFE
Look at that. *That's* very strange...isn't it?

NARRATOR
What is that?

WIFE
Why...it looks as if someone carved this dark patch into the plaster...

NARRATOR
It looks like...

WIFE
A cat.

NARRATOR

What's *that* thing there?

WIFE

It looks like...a rope. A rope about the animal's neck.

NARRATOR

A...*rope,* you say?

(MUSIC)

"At first, I was trembling. But, then I thought, the cat had been hanged in the garden, not the bedroom. Sure, what had *this* to do with that?"

WIFE

How did it get there on the wall?

NARRATOR

How did it get there? "Well, using the best of logic, I somehow concocted a scenario that included the heat of fire, the ashes of burnt wood, a beam falling against the wall, leaving a blackened scar, an imprint, stained from water thrown on the fire... *that,* together with our imaginations, resembled a hanged cat."

(END OF MUSIC)

It's just an optical trick that occurred from a combination of coincidences. You know, the way people are always seeing religious figures in a tree trunk, or on wet pavement?

(MUSIC)

"That might have solved the mystery for the moment, but, it did not, altogether, satisfy me. For months I could not rid myself of the image of the cat. I began to miss my old friend. Every time I went to the tavern, I looked about me, down the street, around the corner, for Pluto. I'd even looked for another cat to replace him. One night as I sat, half-stupefied, in the tavern...I found myself staring off into the shadows, into the far corner where the barrels were stored...and *there*, sitting on top of a stack of kegs...I saw something black...*a black cat!* As big as old Pluto! I approached it. It surely did look like him...except that Pluto was pure black. This cat had a large splotch of white on his breast.

(END OF MUSIC. CAT PURRS)

Well now…who are you then? Do you have an owner? If not, would you like to come home with me? Landlord? Is this your cat?"

LANDLORD

No. I've never seen it before.

NARRATOR

Aha…alright, my new found friend. Do you want to come with me?

(MUSIC)

"I didn't even have to pick it up. The cat followed me home. And, he made himself right at home. My wife took to him immediately. But, wouldn't you know? A week passes and I no longer have that good feeling for it. I begin to dislike it, actually. I don't know why. It loves me. But, I begin to become disgusted and annoyed with it. Sure, I even hate it. I avoid the creature. Of course, it reminds me of my guilt and shame, my former cruelty to Pluto. But, now…I can't bear to be in the same room with it.

"Why? I hadn't noticed while I was drunk in the tavern and brought the beast home…but, when my mind was a bit clearer, I could see…like Pluto, this cat has only one eye. My wife, having never known the true facts about what had happened to Pluto, loves this poor thing even more so. I wish I could be my old self. Maybe, I might feel the same sympathy for it. But, I don't. The more I try to avoid the cat, the more it clings to my heels, following me everywhere. If I sit, it's under my chair. Or leaping up on my lap, caressing me.

(CAT PURRS)

"If I walk, it gets between my feet, nearly tripping me. Sometimes, it claws its way up my pants leg to my shirt just to sit on my chest. I want to knock it down with my fist. But, I don't…I remember what I had done to Pluto. Alright, I admit… I am deadly afraid of this creature. I'm scared that it will do some harm to me. I can't explain the fear."

(MUSIC ENDS)

WIFE
Have you seen, taken a good look, at the white spot on this cat? On its chest?

NARRATOR
Why? What about it?

WIFE
Well, when you brought it home...it was just a big white shape.

NARRATOR
Yeah...and?

WIFE
Well, if you look at it now...it looks definitely like something...

NARRATOR
Like...what?

WIFE
Well...what are those things on which they hang people? The gallows!

NARRATOR
Are you kidding me?

WIFE
No! Look at it. That's what it looks like...a gallows.

NARRATOR
You're crazy. It doesn't look like a gallows.

(MUSIC)

"But, it does. I can see it plain as day. Now, I am frightened even more. What does it mean? Can it be some sort of message from beyond? But, Pluto was just a cat, a dumb beast. He didn't have a soul. He wasn't created in God's image. Now, I'm a nervous wreck. I barely sleep. My dreams became nightmares. I wake up screaming...*aaahhh!*

(CAT GROWLS)

"Only to find the hot breath of that *thing* upon my face, sitting on my chest, right over my beating heart and I am powerless to shake it off. It's tormenting me so much...the last bit of good that is within me disappears, giving way to the darkest and most *evil* of thoughts. I now hate all things, all mankind. Even my wife. Since the fire, we've been living in a cellar in an old building. Poor as beggars. And, don't think she fails to remind me of that every day. So, a few hours ago...the cat is following me down the steep stairs...causing me to *trip* and nearly break my neck."

(MUSIC ENDS)

You're trying to kill me, aren't you! Where is that axe? There it is! I'll fix you, you no good, rotten...

WIFE
Just what do you think you're going to do with that?

NARRATOR
Leave my wrist go! Who are you to interfere?

WIFE
Put it down!

NARRATOR
Leave me alone or I'll....!

WIFE
Stop! Murder! *Aaahhhhhh!*

(THUD)

NARRATOR
"Well, now you've done it. You killed her. You killed your wife. You buried the axe in her head and now her brains are all over the cellar floor. I didn't mean to...she got in the way. She saw that you were angry. She saw you with the ax. She shouldn't have gotten in the way. What are you going to do now? Confess? Go to the police? Don't be ridiculous. They'll never believe you that it was an accident. You have to hide her, of course. You have to...

(MUSIC)

"Think! *Think!* You can't remove it from the house without the risk of being observed by the neighbors. There must be some other way. Maybe, maybe...you can cut the corpse up into tiny fragments and throw them into the fire? Or...or...I know...you can dig a grave for her in the floor of the cellar. Or, throw bits of her down the well in the yard. No...what if you packed her in a box and made it to *look* like a regular shipping parcel and you can order a porter to pick it up and...Ah, I know....what if you did what those monks had done to their victims back in the Middle ages? Why not wall her up in the cellar? That can be easily done. The walls are loosely constructed. It's been recently plastered. The dampness has prevented it from hardening. You can simply remove the bricks, insert the corpse, plaster it all up again and no one would be any wiser. Where's that crowbar? Start dislodging the bricks...that's it...

(HAMMERING, BRICKS)

"Next...I'll deposit the body against the inner wall. That's it...prop it up nicely. She'll have to stand. No room to lie down. Now, I'll just start relaying the bricks as they were...and some new plaster should do the job.

(MUSIC ENDS)

"Good as new! A work of art. All cleaned up. Can't tell it's been disturbed in the slightest. But, there's still one thing on my mind. *The cat!* Yes, where is that damned beast? The cause of all my misfortune! It escaped from me when my wife interfered. Well, just wait, I'll do to *you* what I did to her! It might have taken off for good. Just as well. I can finally have a good night's sleep for myself.

(MUSIC)

"Well, it's been what? Two days, three days? And still my tormentor hasn't shown itself. Looks like I'm a free man. Let's hope it's gone forever. For the first time, in a long time, I am a happy man. I'm not even feeling guilty over what I've done. To cover my tracks, I've even notified the police that my wife is missing...perhaps, she's taken off with a lover? But, they're coming now to inspect the premises. Of course, they'll find nothing.

(KNOCK)

"There they are now."

(DOOR OPEN)

SHERIFF

Good day. I am Sheriff Knox. Here are my credentials. I understand that you have reported that your wife is missing? Do you mind if we come in and have a look around? Purely, to complete our records and then we'll be out of your way.

NARRATOR

Certainly.

SHERIFF

The bureaucracy, you understand? I must apologize, but, if you allow me in, I'll make it quick.

NARRATOR

Of course, come right in.

(DOOR CLOSES, MUSIC)

"They inspect every nook and cranny. I even accompany them. No corner unexplored. Now, they're entering the cellar...well, I'm not even quivering a muscle. My heart is beating as calmly as an innocent man. Let them walk and look wherever they desire."

(MUSIC ENDS)

SHERIFF

Well, everything looks fine to me. We'll be on our way. I'm sorry to have bothered you.

NARRATOR

Any time, Sheriff. I only hope you will be able to find my wife.

SHERIFF

This house...this is a well-constructed house. My parents lived in a house like this. Reminds me of my childhood. They don't make em like this anymore.

NARRATOR

Uhm, yes, that's true...actually, these walls can withstand the test of time. Solid as a rock.

(MUSIC)

"And, now, I do the most *unintelligent* thing in my life. I pick up my cane and rap on the wall, the very portion of brickwork behind which stands the corpse of my wife. As soon as I do that, I realize that the Sheriff might hear that this particular wall is not as solid as a rock...but. rather hollow. Yet, it's *not* the sound of a hollow wall which draws his attention..."

(MUFFLED CAT HOWL)

SHERIFF

What's that?

NARRATOR

What? I...don't hear anything.

SHERIFF

It's...a...cat...inside the wall.

(CAT SCREAMING GROWS LOUDER)

NARRATOR

"At first, it's muffled and broken, like the sobbing of a child, but, now, it's quickly swelling into one long, loud, and continuous scream, half of horror and half of triumph, like something out of Hell...the sound of the damned in their agony and of the demons that exult in their damnation! I feel like I'm going to faint. I stagger to the opposite wall. For one instant, the Sheriff and his police remain motionless, terrified, awestruck. What are they going to do?"

SHERIFF

Men! *Tear down that wall!*

(HAMMERS, CRASH, MUSIC)

NARRATOR

"In minutes, the wall falls. The corpse, already greatly decayed and clotted with gore, stands erect before our eyes. Upon its head, with red extended mouth and solitary eye of fire, sits the hideous beast whose craft had seduced me into murder, and whose terrible voice now consigns me to the hangman. You stupid fool! You stupid, *stupid* fool! You had walled up the monster *within the tomb!*"

(MUSIC ENDS)

LET LOOSE
By Dan Bianchi
From A Story By Mary Cholmondeley

Cast – 2m, 2w
Length – 20 min
Synopsis – An artist spends time in a haunted crypt

RITA

Phew, it's a hot one today. Temperature must be hitting ninety five. And yet...here you are, dressed as if we're going to a grand ball...

CHARLES

You know I'm a slave to fashion.

RITA

But, we're out hiking now. No need for three piece suits and...how on Earth are you coping with that old fashioned, starched collar? Why do you wear them?

CHARLES

Do you really want to know?

RITA

Why not? We've all the time in the world.

CHARLES

Well...ten years ago, I was asked to write a paper on English Frescoes at the Institute of British Architects. I was determined to make the paper as good as I could, down to the slightest details, and I consulted many books on the subject, and studied every fresco I could find. There was one in particular...the east wall of a crypt in a parish church up in Yorkshire. I decided to go there and see the fresco for myself. I brought my dog, Brian, the Golden Retriever...you remember him?

RITA

Oh, sure. Brian.

CHARLES

Good old Brian. Well...I get to Yorkshire...the church is in a tiny, out of the way village called, get this...Wet Waste On The Wolds.

RITA

Wet Waste On The...*Wolds?*

CHARLES

Don't ask. I travel by train and, then, an additional ten miles by horse cart and, *then*, by foot over the moors. It's night when I reach the place and I have considerable difficulty in getting any one to take me in. But, I find a bed in the tavern. It has a little stream running right outside the window.

RITA

How quaint.

CHARLES

Well, you can't imagine how *rural* Wet Waste is...a straggling row of one-story grey stone houses...In fact, everything is grey. The fences, the little bridges at either end of town, the walls. All stone grey. There's the church...

RITA

Grey?

CHARLES

Of course. There's also a mob of rough, uncouth children, who eye me and Brian with half-defiant curiosity.

RITA

They don't throw any grey rocks at you, do they?

CHARLES

I don't give them a chance. I rush along to the clergyman's house and meet the old man who is perusing over his papers and books.

PASTOR

Mister, er...?

CHARLES

Blake. Charles Blake.

PASTOR

Blake.

CHARLES

Remember? I wrote to you? I'm an architect. I've come to study a fresco in the crypt of your church and I'll need the keys.

PASTOR

The crypt? The crypt has been closed for thirty years. Ever since…

CHARLES

I shouldn't be long. But, I'll need the keys.

PASTOR

No, no…no one goes in there now.

CHARLES

But, you wrote back to me…told me to come.

PASTOR

I did?

CHARLES

I've come a long way. I've an important paper I had been asked to read at Oxford and…I can really use the fresco as a…

PASTOR

Ah! I can understand that. I also was young once, and fired with ambition. But, my mission has taken me to a somewhat lonely place, and, for forty years, I have held in my hands the curing of souls here…truly, I have seen but little of the world, though I, myself. am most interested in the paths of literature. Possibly, you may have read a pamphlet, written by myself, on the Syrian version of the Three Authentic Epistles of Ignatius?

CHARLES

I am ashamed to confess that I have not time to read even the most celebrated books. My one object in life is my art. Ars longa, vita brevis, you know.

PASTOR

You are right, my son. There are diversities of gifts, and, if the Lord has entrusted you with a talent, look to it. Lay it not up in a napkin.

CHARLES

No. So, if you'd just lend me the keys to the crypt...

PASTOR

Well...I don't know...hmmm...oh, why not? You appear to be a good youth. And superstition! What is it, but, distrust in God? They are here in the cupboard. They should be here. Years of dust in here. See, my son, if among these parchments there be two keys... one of iron and very large, and the other steel, and of a long thin appearance.

CHARLES

Let's see...ah yes, are these the ones?

PASTOR

Those are them. The long one opens the first door at the bottom of the steps which go down against the outside wall of the church hard by the sword graven in the wall. The second opens the iron door within the passage leading to the crypt itself. My son, is it truly necessary to your treatise that you should enter this crypt?

CHARLES

Absolutely.

PASTOR

Then take them. And in the evening you will bring them to me again.

CHARLES

I may be here for several days. Can I keep them until my work is finished?

PASTOR
No. You must return them each night. And, you must be careful that you lock the first door at the foot of the steps before you unlock the second, and, lock the second also while you are within. Furthermore, when you come out… promise me that you'll lock the iron inner door, as well as, the wooden one.

CHARLES
I promise.

RITA
Well, sounds like you got your keys.

CHARLES
Now, Brian is waiting for me on the porch. I grab my sketching materials and off I go to the church. The church itself is interesting. It was built on top of the ruins of an earlier church. There are still early carvings in the walls. Incised crosses, and swords.
(FOOTSTEPS DESCEND,
LOCK OPENS, DOOR CREAKS OPEN)

The entrance to the crypt is a flight of narrow steps green with moss and mildew. Damp and slippery. Brian is with me every step of the way. He's not staying behind. We get to the bottom, in near darkness…
(STRIKES MATCH)

and I have to strike a light before I can find the keyhole and the proper key to fit into it.
(DOOR CREAKS)

As instructed, I carefully lock it behind me… although I'd prefer to leave it open. Just in case.

NARRATOR
Just in case.
(CRYPT SOUNDS, DRIPPING, HOLLOW ECHO)

CHARLES
It's difficult to keep the candle lit. I have to feel my way down a low passage to the next door.

(TOAD CROAKS)

A big fat toad is just sitting there, in front of the door, as if he's guarded it for a hundred years. The door. The iron door.
(OPENS LOCK, OPENS IRON
DOOR, WIND)

I feel... the cold breath of the crypt upon my face. And once again, I must lock myself in.
(DOOR SHUTS, LOCKS DOOR)

RITA

So, what do you see?

CHARLES

I am standing in a low vaulted chamber cut out of solid rock. I can't see the end of it in this darkness. There are other rough archways... probably served at one time for family vaults. And...

RITA

And...?

CHARLES

Skulls and bones... packed about four feet high on either side. Not just piles, but, skillfully arranged.

RITA

And, the fresco?

CHARLES

I look round for it. Where can it be? I wander into a second smaller chamber. I hold up my candle and...there it is. The fresco.

RITA

What does it look like?

CHARLES

As soon as I lay eyes on it, I know it is unique. I can't wait to examine it closely.

RITA

How old is it?

CHARLES

Early fifteenth century. But, it's perfectly preserved. I can still see the trowel marks in the plaster. It's a picture of the Ascension, gloriously treated. I'm trembling with joy. It's a magnificent specimen of English fresco painting...and I will be the one to make it known to the world. I light a dozen candles and get to work sketching.

(DOG GROWLS)

"Brian! What's wrong with you? Getting spooked, boy? Here, here's a biscuit." So, after working for several hours, I pause to rest my eyes and hands and I notice for the first time the intense stillness that surrounds me. I can't even hear the church bells on the hour. All is silent as the grave.

RITA

Well, technically, you're *in* a grave.

CHARLES

True. Those who had come here have indeed gone down into silence. Gone down into silence. What's that? A faint sound...coming from the vaults...deep underground.

RITA

Bats?

CHARLES

I don't know. What do bats sound like?

RITA

They sound like rats, I imagine. Only up in the air.
(DISTANT THUMP, KEYS JANGLING)

The keys! I've left them in the lock! Why did I do that? I take my candle and make my way back to the iron door...I can tell you, I'm trembling with fear...more noise?

(SHUFFLING)

Something moving. In great haste, I'd say. Look, the key...it's still in the door, but the other key is swinging upon the ring …it's moving, as if it's been touched.

                    RITA
Well, that isn't good.

                    CHARLES
That's it. I'm putting both of them into my pocket. I return to work.

                    RITA
How can you do that? I'd be out of there in a flash.

                    CHARLES
Oh well now…remember the thump I heard? Well, I turn to find a *skull* lying in the middle of the floor. Evidently, it just slipped from its place on the top of one of the walls of bones, and had rolled almost to my feet.

                    RITA
And, how did it do that after it's been there for a hundred years or more?

                    CHARLES
A draft from the open door…or the vibrations from the iron door closing? I'm thinking of returning it to its place, but, better not risk all of them tumbling down. I'm not about to start gathering up scattered teeth.

                    RITA
Right. Leave it alone. Go back to work.

                    CHARLES
Which is what I do until my candles start to run out. Poor Brian can't wait to get out. As I open the iron door, he pushes past me and starts scratching at the wooden door. Once out into sunlight…well, you can imagine. Hard to believe that such a place exists down below our feet. I return the keys to the parson and dine at the local inn. It's a lonely place up there. Pretty wild. The people still live a rural, primitive life. I don't think they even read any newspapers to know what's going on

in the world. And their dialect? You'd be hard pressed to understand a word of it. Now...here's where the strange part of my story begins...

RITA

Oh? The strange part?

CHARLES

So, I'm sitting there in the inn...and a pretty little girl comes in with golden hair and she sits down and I begin to sketch some animals and birds and she enjoys it so much, I'm soon surrounded by a crowd of children. And, adults.

RITA

So, you're a hit with the locals?

CHARLES

Not really. You see...the next morning, I find that the village is buzzing with chatter and people are staring in the windows of the inn and I can hear a woman crying in the distance. Even the woman who brings me my breakfast is in tears..."What's wrong?" I ask. "What happened?" What do you think she says? "Oh, sir...the neighbor's child, the little girl for whom you made those pictures...she died in the night."

RITA

Oh my God!

CHARLES

My heart drops a beat. I'm speechless. All I can do is grab my gear and head for the crypt. The day passes without any disturbances. Even Brian sleeps at my feet on the cold stone floor. When I return the keys at night, the pastor asks me to have tea with him.

PASTOR

And, has the work prospered?

CHARLES

Yes, oh yes. Here, here are my drawings. You have seen the original fresco, of course?

PASTOR

Once. Long ago. When I was young, forty years ago, and came here because I had no means of mine own, and was much moved to marry at that time, I felt oppressed that all was so old... and that this place was so far removed from the world, from which I had, at times, longed to escape. But, I had chosen my lot, and, with it, I was forced to be content. My son, marry not in youth, for love, which truly in that season is a mighty power, turns away the heart from study, and young children break the back of ambition. Neither marry in middle life, when a woman is seen to be but a woman, and, her talk a weariness, so you will not be burdened with a wife in your old age.

RITA

Sage advice. So, how did you answer him?

CHARLES

I didn't. Let him have his opinions.

PASTOR

Yes, all about here is old. The paved road leading to Dyke Fens is an ancient pack road, made even in the time of the Romans. Likewise, old and forgotten by the world. The Reformation never reached Dyke Fens. It stopped here. Do you know that they still have a priest and a bell, and bow down before the saints? It is a damnable heresy, and, weekly, I expound it as such to my people, showing them true doctrines... and I have heard that this same priest has so far yielded himself to the Evil One... that,he has preached against me as withholding gospel truths from my flock. But I take no heed of it.

CHARLES

The following morning I go for the keys for the third and last time. I've decided to leave early the next day. I'm tired of Wet Waste On The Wolds. I feel as if...there's trouble in the air. Something brewing. A storm coming on.

RITA

I get the point. Continue...

CHARLES

But, this morning...to my astonishment...

PASTOR

My son, I know why you have come, but, it is of no avail. I cannot lend the keys again.

CHARLES

I just need them *one* more time, Pastor.

PASTOR

It is impossible. I did wrong, exceedingly wrong. I will never part with them again.

CHARLES

Why not?

PASTOR

Well...The old clerk, Abraham Kelly, died last night. The doctor has just been here to tell me of that which is a mystery to him. I do not wish the people of the place to know it... and only to me he has mentioned it... but, he has discovered plainly on the throat of the old man...and, also, but more faintly on the child's throat... *marks* as of strangulation. None, but, he has observed it, and, he is at a loss how to account for it. I, alas, *can* account for it, but, in one way... but, in one way!

CHARLES

That's terrible, Pastor. If there is a murderer on the loose, he must be caught. Still, I don't see what all *this* has to do with the crypt.

PASTOR

It is a long story, and, to a stranger, it may appear but foolishness, but, I will tell it... for, I perceive that, unless I furnish a reason for withholding the keys, you will not cease asking. I told you, at first, when you inquired of me concerning the crypt, that, it had been closed these thirty years, and, so it was. Thirty years ago a certain *Sir Roger Despard* departed this life. He was the Lord of the manor of Wet Waste and Dyke Fens, the last of his family, which is, now, thank the Lord, extinct. He was a vile man. Feared neither God nor man. He suffered many vices, more especially from drunkenness. They say he was possessed by seven devils, being an abomination to his household and a root of bitterness to all, both high and low. At last, he faced death. I went to hear his final words on his death-bed. I found a man terrified, filled with evil imaginations. Even as I was there to hear his repentance, he did nothing, but, scoff at me and my beliefs, even as he lay dying...

ROGER

Get out of here, with your superstitious claptrap! There is no God...no angels! *No bloody Heaven!* Don't you know? We're *all* damned. Me, you, *everyone!*

PASTOR

Evening came and he raved even more...

ROGER

I am being strangled by that Evil One! *Strangled*...can't breathe...

PASTOR

Now, on his table was his hunting knife, and with his last strength, he crept and laid hold upon it and swore a great oath...

ROGER

If I go down to burn in hell, I'll leave one of my hands behind on this Earth. It'll never rest until it's drawn blood from the throat of another...*strangling him*...even as I am now being strangled!

PASTOR

And, then...he cut off his own right hand at the wrist, and no man dared go near him to stop him, and the blood went through the floor, even down to the ceiling of the room below, and, thereupon, he died. And, they called me in the night, and told me of his oath...I thought it better he should take it with him, so that he might have it. No man should speak of it...

CHARLES

He cut off his hand?

PASTOR

I took the severed hand, which none had ventured to touch, and I laid it beside him in his coffin... if some day after much tribulation he should perchance be moved to stretch forth his hands towards God. But, the story got spread about, and the people were frightened, so, when he came to be buried in the place of his fathers, he, being the last of his family, and the crypt likewise full, I had it closed... and kept the keys myself, and suffered no man to enter, therein, any more.... for truly he was a man of an evil life, and the devil is not yet wholly overcome, nor cast chained into the lake of fire. In time the story died out, for in thirty years much is forgotten. And when you came and asked me for the keys, I was, at the first, minded to withhold them... but I thought it was a vain superstition... these are modern times, no? So, I let you have them, seeing it was not an idle curiosity, but, a desire to improve the talent committed to you.

CHARLES
Surely, Pastor, one so cultivated and deeply read as yourself cannot be biased by an idle superstition?

PASTOR
I trust not and, yet...it is a strange thing that, since the crypt was opened. two people have died, and the mark is plain upon the throat of the old man and visible on the young child. No blood was drawn, but, the second time, the grip was stronger than the first. The third time...?

CHARLES
Superstition such as that...is an entire want of faith in God. You once said so yourself.

PASTOR
True. What *is* faith?

CHARLES
Besides, if...if...there is some malign influence that has been *let loose* since my first day down there...well, it's out now for good or evil. My coming and going in the crypt won't make much difference.

RITA
Did that work?

CHARLES

Yes. I nearly wrestled them out of his hand. I rushed to the crypt and locked myself in.

(CRYPT SOUNDS, DRIPPING, ECHO)

This time...*the silence*...I notice it again. That place, that hole where the skull had fallen from...it's big enough I can pass my hand into it. And, for the first time I notice...a carved coat-of-arms, and the name, now almost obliterated, of Despard.

RITA

So, *this* is the Despard vault?

CHARLES

Yes. I move a few more skulls, making that hole larger. What can be behind it? I put my candle into the aperture...the vault was full. Piled high, one upon another, filled with old coffins, and remnants of coffins, and strewn bones. And, *there* is the coffin of Sir Roger...*wicked* Sir Roger...with a large crack across its lid.

RITA

What did you do?

CHARLES

Well, I put back the skulls, that's what I do. Including the one which had fallen out. An hour later, I finish my work. And, I'm back out into the sunshine, planning to leave that godforsaken place as soon as possible. But, that's not possible...the only train that stops at Pickering has already come and gone for today. So, Brian and I wander about for the remainder of the afternoon. In the evening, in my room, I work on my writing. Working quickly, as if, I'm pressed for time. I write and write, until my candles run low.

(CLOCK CHIMES)

Time for bed. Instead, I sit down by the open window and lean out to try and catch a breath of air. It's a beautiful night. But, terribly warm. The moon is a perfect circle illuminating the whole village as if in broad daylight. I should be happy I am leaving this place...instead, I'm overtaken by a great depression. I'm thinking of that crypt and the countless dead who had been laid there. I wasn't affected within the crypt, but, now, it suddenly hits me…What is the good of working and toiling, and grinding down my heart and youth? For what reason? It all ends in the same place…the grave. Even if I succeed, after a life of toil…what remains for me in the end? The grave. A little sooner, while the hands and eyes are still strong to work… or a little later, when all power and vision have been taken from them… sooner or later, only…the grave.

RITA
My oh my…aren't we morbid?

CHARLES
Maybe, it's the full moon affecting me.   Might as well go to bed. I don't know how long I sleep, but…

(DOG GROWLS)

"Brian! What's wrong, boy? Shush! You'll wake the whole house. Quiet, boy!"   I can see him in the moonlight…

RITA
What's he doing?

CHARLES
He's staring at something…in the air. "Brian, there's nothing there, boy."   Is he going mad? His eyes are glaring, his teeth bared…he's following the movement of something, something moving quickly.

(WILD BARKING)

With a furious snarl, he suddenly springs from the ground, and rushes in great leaps across the room towards me

(FURNITURE CRASH)

dashing himself against the furniture, his eyes rolling, snatching and tearing wildly in the air with his teeth.

RITA
He *has* gone mad!

CHARLES
I leap out of bed, and rush at him, catching him by the collar.

The moon has gone behind a cloud…

(GROWLING, STRUGGLE)

but, in the darkness I feel him turn upon me, feel him rise up, and his teeth close in my throat. I'm being strangled! With all the strength of despair, I grip his neck, and, drag him across the room, trying to crush his head against the iron rail of my bed. It's my only chance. There's blood running down my neck. I'm suffocating. In the next instance…I beat his head against the bar and hear his skull give way. He gives one strong shudder, a groan… and then… I faint away.

RITA

Dear God…I had no idea…

CHARLES

When I come to, I'm lying on the floor, surrounded by the people of the house, my reddened hands still clutching Brian's throat. Someone is holding a candle towards me, and the draft from the window makes it flare and waver. I look at Brian. My poor Brian. Stone dead. The blood from his battered head is trickling slowly over my hands. His great jaw is fixed in something that…in the uncertain light…I cannot see. But, when they turn the light a little… Oh, God! There! Look! Look!

PASTOR

Son…Charles? Look, he's fainted again…

CHARLES

The old Pastor carefully nurses me back to health…the people of the village are caring and concerned, as well. The doctor came…I told him what I had seen…what I had done.

PASTOR

Rest assured, you suffered some sort of hallucination, lad. The mind plays terrible tricks…especially you having seen your dog go mad.

CHARLES

Pastor, did you see the dog after it was dead?

PASTOR

That I did. The whole jaw was covered with blood and foam...the teeth certainly seemed convulsively fixed...I'd say this is a case of virulent hydrophobia...an extreme case... owing to the intense heat. I had the dog buried immediately.

(MUSIC)

CHARLES

So...now you know why I wear these old fashioned high neck starched collars.

RITA

I do?

CHARLES

You see I have the marks still....but, I have no fear of dying of hydrophobia. I am told such peculiar scars could not have been made by the teeth of a dog. If you look closely you can see the pressure of the five fingers. That is the reason why I wear high collars.

THE THING IN THE HALL
By Dan Bianchi
From A Story By E. F. Benson

Cast - 2m
Length - 15 min
Synopsis - Two men discover a dangerous spirit

(MUSIC)

NARRATOR
"Both Louis Fielder and I attended Harvard together. Friends for forty years. Two totally different kinds of people. At thirty-five, I became a renowned authority on functions and diseases of the brain. Louis, although a brilliant fellow, still hasn't achieved much of anything. He spends too much time investigating whatever interests him and assigning theories to abstract problems. And, before he finishes with one project, he's on to the next. Still, we have one thing in common...we both have an insatiable curiosity after the unknown and we're not afraid to go after it. I'd sit next to a bubonic plague victim to gauge the progression of the disease. He'd study X-rays one week, flying machines the next, and spiritualism after that. When I returned from Europe, he begged me to set up my practice in a house next to his, downtown, while most doctors of any note congregate midtown."

LOUIS
Bah! *Midtown?* That's Chloroform Square! All those old biddies passing themselves off as medical experts? Sure, they'll prolong your life... as long as they can make their money. But, they don't do much to make people live. I mean, *really live!* Anyway, who cares *where* a doctor lives, so long as he cures people? Besides, *you* don't believe in old methods... why believe in old localities? Live next to me in Chelsea and I can drop in from time to time.

NARRATOR
"Of course, I remember whenever Louis said *drop in* it meant three A.M. and he'd stay for hours talking about everything and anything. But, I was new in town, so, I thought it would be nice to live next to someone I know. Well, one night, I was visiting

him at his house...at a reasonable time, of course, when..."
                                        (KNOCKS)

That's a loud door knocker you've got there, Louis.

                    LOUIS
I don't have a door knocker. But, you heard that, didn't you?

                    NARRATOR
Of course! It must have been the mailman dropping off letters.

                    LOUIS
No, it's not the mailman. It was the *Thing.*

                    NARRATOR
Oh? What *Thing?*

                    LOUIS
I don't really know. That's what makes it so interesting. Some
may claim it's from the other world beyond death.

                    NARRATOR
Personally, I detest and despise the whole notion of
spiritualism. No, there's a simpler explanation for it, I'm sure.
It's probably the mailman. I'll look for myself.
                                        (DOOR OPENS)

                    LOUIS
Anything?

                    NARRATOR
No...no one here. No mail either.
                                        (DOOR CLOSE)

                    LOUIS
Have you ever tried table-turning? It's rather odd.

                    NARRATOR
Now, what are you on to? Table turning?

                    LOUIS
You study the powers of the brain. Do you think you can move

that table using mental strength alone?

NARRATOR

That kind of thinking leads people to believe they can cure cancer with tea leaves.

LOUIS

Oh come on. You didn't believe in hypnotism at all when you went to Paris. Now, you're a devout believer, no?

NARRATOR

It does help to cure certain mental illnesses.

LOUIS

Try its weight. See if you can push it about.

NARRATOR

Alright. *Hmmph!* Okay, it's a very heavy table.

LOUIS

Now, put your hands on the top of it and see what you can do.

NARRATOR

This is a waste of time...

LOUIS

Just do it.

NARRATOR

Okay, nothing...see? I'd much rather play chess or even talk about politics, than turn tables.

LOUIS

Now, let us both put our fingers only on top of the table and push for all we are worth, from right to left. Go ahead, push! That's it...more now...

NARRATOR

I'm pushing! Ah...forget it. It isn't moving.

(KNOCKS)

Listen! There's that rapping again.

LOUIS

I told you. It's the Thing. Alright, let me draw the curtains.
Let's make it as dark as possible in here. There now. We've
only the light from the flames in the fireplace. Now, put your
hands on the table...quite lightly, and, how shall I say it
...*expect.*

NARRATOR

Expect? Expect what? This is silly, Louis.

LOUIS

Shush! Wait...wait...there! Do you feel that? In your
fingertips?

NARRATOR

You're being totally...oh! Why...yes...*yes,* I do.

LOUIS

A faint vibration...growing stronger...like water boiling in a
kettle. Getting stronger...*listen!*

(HUMMING NOISE)

Do you hear that?

NARRATOR

(Whispers) The table is *moving!* Revolving on its own...

LOUIS

Keep your hands on it and move with it. There now...here we
go...move with it, move...that's it...quiet now. Are you there?

NARRATOR

Who are you talking to?

(LOUD KNOCK)

Alright, that was loud. Where did it come from?

(LOUD KNOCKS ECHO. THEN SILENCE)

(Whispers) I can't see a thing. Can you? Oh wait, what's that?
I see a light or something...a speck of light...you didn't strike a
match, did you?

(LOUD BOOM)

LOUIS

I think…it's gone. I'll open the curtains now.

NARRATOR

Yes, please do. So, what was *that* all about? Don't tell me…
that was what one calls a *séance,* right? Am I to believe we
were just visited by a spirit from another world?

LOUIS

I can't say. This was the fifth time I've experienced it.
Sometimes, they come on their own. Sometimes, I call to them
as you have just witnessed.

NARRATOR

So, that makes you a *medium*, I suppose? And, those little
lights?

LOUIS

I don't know what they are. I have no control of them…or any
of it.

NARRATOR

Hmmm. I guess I should start spouting theories involving the
unconscious self…the vast majority of our deeds spring,
apparently without volition, from this unconscious self. We are
just beginning to learn how much it plays in the life of man. All
hearing is the unconscious exercise of the aural nerve, all
seeing of the optic, all walking, all ordinary movement seem to
be done without the exercise of will on our part.

LOUIS

I don't know about that.

NARRATOR

If we take up some new form of progression, skating, for
instance, the beginner will learn with falls and difficulty the
outside edge, but, within a few hours of his having learned his
balance on it, he will give no more thought to what he learned
so short a time ago as an acrobatic feat, than he gives to the
placing of one foot before the other.

LOUIS
Well, you're a brain specialist. I *expect* to hear that gobbledy gook from a psychiatrist, *not* a surgeon. As I said before, you didn't believe in hypnotism until you learned more about it. How can you deny that what you just witnessed isn't a form of spiritualism?

NARRATOR
What I saw and heard and what you saw and heard was an exhibition of thought-transference, which, in all my experience, I must admit, I've never seen surpassed. I know that I am, myself, extremely sensitive to suggestion, and my part in it this evening I believe to be purely that of the *receiver* of suggestions... so vivid that I visualized and heard these phenomena which existed only in *your* brain.

LOUIS
Nonsense! That *Thing* was trying to communicate with us. It didn't come from my mind. It moved the table...*made noises* ...made streaks of light.

NARRATOR
Yes, but, by the *Thing*...what do you mean? Is it a long past great-uncle returning from the grave? Was it a spirit? *Whose* spirit?

LOUIS
No. I don't think it is great-uncle anybody. I don't *know*, as I told you, what the *Thing* is. But, if you ask me what I *think* it is...that Thing is an Elemental.

NARRATOR
Oh? And, what is an Elemental?

LOUIS
There are good things in this world, are there not, and bad things? Cancer, I take it, is bad, and...and fresh air is good. Honesty is good, lying is bad. Impulses of some sort direct both sides, and some power suggests the impulses. Well, I went into this spiritualistic business, impartially. I learned to expect... to throw open the door into the soul, and I said, "Anyone may come in." And, I think... something has applied

for admission...that *Thing* that tapped and turned the table and lit up, as you saw, yourself. Now, the control of the evil principle in the world is in the hands of a power which entrusts its errands to the things which I call Elementals. I welcome Elementals. I do not ask only *good* spirits to come in. I don't want hymns played on a music box or a piano. I don't even want an Elemental, necessarily. I only throw open the door. I believe the Thing has come into my house and is establishing communication with me. So, I'm here to do just that. What is it? *Who cares?* I don't care if it's Satan himself, I just want to know.

(MUSIC, WIND)

The window!   The wind...

(GLASS CRASH)

NARRATOR
It's freezing! Louis, I'm so cold...

LOUIS
Look, the wind...it's moving across the room...it's at the fire place. Fanning the flames...

NARRATOR
It'll burn down the house!

LOUIS
(Pause) It's gone now.

NARRATOR
The Elemental has gone up the chimney?

LOUIS
Oh, no, the Thing only passed us by. It's not gone. Look, what's that? *There* on the wall. A shadow...

NARRATOR
And, it's moving. What is it, Louis?

LOUIS
It's not shaped like man nor beast. Like some enormous *slug*...is that a head?

NARRATOR

Looks like a seal or a walrus. With a long tongue hanging out of its mouth. *If* that's a mouth.

(LOUD KNOCK ECHOES)

LOUIS

Well, I said I was ready for anything. She's a beauty, isn't she?

(MUSIC)

NARRATOR

"Now, I was still, even in spite of the appearance of this shadow, quite convinced that I was only taking observations of a most curious case of disordered brain accompanied by the most vivid and remarkable thought-transference. I believed that I had not seen a slug-like shadow at all, but, that, Louis had visualized this dreadful creature so intensely that *I* saw what *he* saw. I've done a bit of reading on the subject since then. That shadow, whatever it was, seems to be a common form for Elementals to take. Louis must have known that and conjured it up in his mind. In any case, for the next six months, we watched and waited, but, neither the Thing, nor the shadow, appeared again. I began to feel it was a waste of time."

LOUIS

Why don't we get a *real* medium in here? You can induce hypnotic sleep, and see if we can learn anything further.

NARRATOR

"So, we did just that. The medium, a young man, sat between Louis and myself, and without the slightest difficulty I put him into a light hypnotic sleep. Five…ten minutes passed, when…"

(LOUD KNOCKS ECHO)

LOUIS

Look! The shadow! It looks as if it's glowing…smoldering…

NARRATOR

"At that moment the medium's face became contorted to a mask of hellish terror… mouth and eyes were both open, and the eyes were focused on something close to him. The Thing, waving its head, came closer and closer to him, and reached out towards his throat. Then, he cried out…

(MAN SCREAMS)

"And, he sprang up, but, it had already caught hold, and for the moment he could not get free."

LOUIS

We have to help him!

NARRATOR

"My hands touched something cold and slimy. But, pull as we could, we could *not* get it away. We could not get a firm grip on it! It felt like slimy fur...the touch of it was horrible, *unclean!* I still couldn't believe it, yet, I reached out to the electric switch on the wall nearby...and turned it on!

(MUSIC)

"Louis was kneeling beside the medium on the floor. The young man's face was drained, white as a sheet. On his throat...two scratches, blood dripping down his neck. Still in hypnotic sleep, I woke him. He put his hand to his throat and found it bleeding, but, as I expected, knew nothing of what had passed."

LOUIS

There was, indeed...an unusual manifestation...while in sleep, you wrestled with something. I'm sorry for this, but, I must thank you, wholeheartedly, for your participation.

(MUSIC)

NARRATOR

"I never saw the young man again. I am told, a week after that instance, he died of blood-poisoning. That only fueled Louis onward to continue his exploration into the world of spirits. He was convinced that the Thing had eventually materialized into solid form. The huge slug, the Elemental, manifested itself no longer by knocks and moving tables, nor, by shadows. It was there in a form that could be *seen* and *felt*. But, still...it only appeared in near darkness. Remember, when I turned on the light...there was nothing but human beings. True, in the struggle, perhaps, the medium had clutched his own throat. And, perhaps, I had grasped Louis' sleeve, he mine."

LOUIS
You don't really believe that, do you?

(MUSIC)

NARRATOR
"Now, even though I had my medical practice to attend to...I found that, no matter how I tried, I could think of nothing else except the occurrence of this strange phenomena. So, in order to refrain from losing my patients...I refused to take part in any further séance with Louis. I had another reason, also. For the last four or five months he was becoming depraved. I have been no prude or Puritan in my own life. But, Louis...he was becoming famous for his immorality. Every club in the city outlawed him. He had been caught several times cheating at cards. He had become cruel...he tortured his cat to death. He had become bestial. Screams had been heard coming from his house. The police had been called. Bloodied women were found. Street whores who refused to press charges. I used to shudder as I passed by his house. I expect some fiendish thing to be looking at me from the window. What could have...?

(DISTANT SCREAMING)

"Now, *that* came from next door. I'm sure of it. So, I run downstairs in my robe and out into the street.

(POLICE WHISTLE)

"The policeman on the beat has heard it too! It's coming from the parlor in Louis' house...we have to break down the door!

(DOOR BREAKING)

"What do we find? It's quiet now. The screaming has ceased. But, there he lies...Louis...quite dead. Both jugulars are severed, torn open. There's blood everywhere.

(MUSIC)

"It's dawn, early and dusky...I'm glad to be back in my house next door to that evil place. I wish I could burn it to the ground and ... *Aaaahhh!* What was that? It's as if...no, it can't be. It felt as if... something seemed to *push* by me, something soft and slimy. It can't be Louis' imagination this time. Yet, I *know* what I felt. There's something here... I know it is. Here, in my house. *There!* No, *there!* Calm down. You're letting your own imagination run away now. Why...you're a man of science, remember that. No matter what you've seen...experienced ...there's always a perfectly clear explanation...

(KNOCKS)

"Oh God! What's that? It can't be...not *here* in my house...
(LOUD POUNDING KNOCKS.
SILENCE)

"It's here. *Here.* Do I see it? Can it be? There it is... in the shadows in the corner of my room... just sitting there... something more substantial than a shadow. Oh yes. The *Thing*...it's here. And now...I can just about see it...yes, it is moving. Moving toward me now... out of the darkness...why can't I run? Why can't I..." Oh, dear God, no! Go away! Go away! *Aaaaahhhhhh!*

THE TOMB OF SARAH
By Dan Bianchi
From A Story By F.G. Loring

Cast - 2m, 1w
Length - 22 min
Synopsis - Two men awaken a centuries old vampire

HUGH
I'm so glad you're here, Joseph. I realize that this is a large commission to restore the chancel of our church at such short notice. It's an historic building, so, we do hope you'll only need to alter things as little as possible. However, the large tomb must be moved ten feet, at least, to the southward.

JOSEPH
It only has one name on it...Sarah, 1630.

HUGH
She was the last of an old family. The Karnsteins have been extinct in these parts for years.

JOSEPH
There's a Latin inscription on it.

HUGH
Yes...but, I'm not sure you'll want to hear it. It reads...*For The Sake Of The Dead And The Welfare Of The Living, Let This Sepulchre Remain Untouched Till The Coming Of Christ.*

JOSEPH
Oh...well...

HUGH
I call it *The Sarah Tomb.* I'd prefer not to have it moved, but, as you can see, the ground beneath it has sunk so much, it's a danger to the safety of the church.

JOSEPH
It shall be moved as reverently as possible. *The Sarah Tomb.* Who was she?

HUGH

There is a local legend that it is the tomb of the evil Countess Sarah, who was murdered in 1630. She lived quite alone in the old castle, whose ruins still stand three miles from here...

JOSEPH

Oh, yes, I've seen it. An evil countess, hey?

HUGH

Her reputation was an evil one even for those days. She was a witch or were-woman. She had a companion, a *familiar* in the shape of a huge Asiatic wolf. This creature was reputed to seize children, or, sheep and other small animals, and convey them to the castle, where the Countess used to suck their blood. It was popularly supposed that she could never be killed. This, however, proved a fallacy, since she was strangled one day by a mad peasant woman who had lost two children, which, she *claimed,* had both been seized and carried off by the Countess's familiar.

JOSEPH

Sounds fantastic! I do love local superstitions. Makes the job a bit more interesting.

HUGH

Now, as you can see, the tomb is made of black marble... there's this enormous slab with these carvings here.

JOSEPH

Hmmm, let's see. It's a beautiful woman reclining on a couch...she does have a rather cruel face. Her mouth open. Oh yes, those are definitely fangs. I take it, *this* is Sarah, herself. Around her neck is a piece of rope, the end of which she holds in her hand. Hmmm, don't know the significance of that. At her side is a gigantic dog with bared fangs and tongue hanging out...her *familiar*, no doubt. Interesting. I've never seen anything like it.

HUGH

Interesting isn't the word for it. It's disgusting. But, historic, so, it must be preserved.

JOSEPH

Well, if we must move the tomb, it will have to be done in two pieces, the covering slab first and, then, the tomb, itself. We'll start tomorrow.

(MUSIC, WORK SOUNDS)

Alright, men...easy on that winch now...is that jack secure? Good. Everyone ready? Good. Let's lift that slab, now. But, easy now, we don't want it to crack in half. We'll all lift on three, slowly now...one, two, *three.*

(WINCH CRANKS)

Hold on a minute...there's some kind of mortar around the seat, it's sealed this pretty tightly...yes, it's an airtight seal. If I can just wedge....Alright, here we go...continue...

(WINCH CRANKS, GUST OF WIND. MEN COUGH)

Oh, dear God in Heaven! What a foul stench! I've never...

HUGH

Look! There she is...Sarah.

JOSEPH

Well, what's left of her. *See!* There, round her neck, a loose cord. There's not much of a neck here, but, there...those marks...she was strangled with it. Or, hanged.

HUGH

But, look at her. Her body. I mean, shouldn't she be nothing but bones by now? It's extraordinary, but...the body hasn't decayed much.

JOSEPH

Yes. And, the way it appears...I don't think it's withered due to old age, but...I'd say she was starved to death. Look here...the flesh is soft and white, the eyes are still intact, wide open...

HUGH

It's frightening, the way they seem to stare at us...almost as...

(MEN GRUMBLE)

Oh, Joseph, the work men...the locals...they're getting a bit...I think they want us to replace the slab.

JOSEPH

Replace it? No, no. We've just started. We've got work to do.
Ivan, we need a temporary cover for the tomb. Use that wood
over there. The rest of you, let's start moving it to its new
place. It must weigh a ton and we have to do this gently.   This
is going to take a couple of days, at least.

(MUSIC, DISTANT DOGS HOWL)

HUGH

Well, it's been two days now. The move has been a success,
no?

JOSEPH

Yes, I'd say so. Oh, that howling, will it never end? What is
going on in the village? Has every dog gone…There, it's
stopped now. I wonder what set them off like that? Strange,
very strange.

HUGH

That's not all that is strange. There's a curious mist that's
risen around the church, have you noticed? Ever since the
tomb has been moved.

JOSEPH

Oh, no, you're *not* suggesting…?

HUGH

Well, according to legend, the disturbance of dogs or wolves at
sunset is supposed to indicate the presence of one of these
fiends…a vampire. Local fog is always considered to be a
certain sign, too.

JOSEPH

Well, you *did* say that the legend made her out to be a vampire
back then.

HUGH

But, this is now. The vampire has the power of producing mist
for the purpose of concealing its movements near its hiding-
place at any time.

JOSEPH

For an educated man, Reverend...you sound like you believe in all this mumbo-jumbo.

(DISTANT DOGS HOWL)

Oh, dear Lord, there they go again.

HUGH

The sun's gone down.

(DISTANT BLOOD CURDLING SCREAM)

JOSEPH

What, in God's name, was that?

HUGH

It came from the church yard! *Look!* Over there! Do you see it?

JOSEPH

What?

HUGH

That dark shape coming out of the mist...it looks like...a huge dog. It's heading out into the field...

JOSEPH

The dogs have stopped...it's gone now.

HUGH

Did you see it? It was a huge dog.

JOSEPH

Yes. I saw it. Reverend, I'm not a hunter, but, even I'd say... *that* was no dog.

(MUSIC)

HUGH

The work men are refusing to work. It seems...a large dog made a raid on their sheep last night. The flock is scattered all over the countryside. Three sheep were found dead , throats ripped out. They're out hunting the beast now. Joseph...I'd like to remove the temporary cover on the tomb and take a look at that mortar…

JOSEPH

The mortar?

HUGH

Yes. Can we lift the wooden lid together? We don't need any of the men?

JOSEPH

Of course. Alright, you take that side…I'll take this side. We'll just slide it this way. Ready? On three…one, two, *three!*
(WOODEN LID SLIDES)

HUGH

Oh, dear Lord!

JOSEPH

My God! She's…*alive!*

HUGH

No, she's not alive. But, she doesn't appear to be withered and…*starved*, any longer, that's for certain. The skin is still a bit wrinkled and shrunken… but, the lips are firm, red, healthy. The eyes…see? More appalling than ever. Still fixed and staring. And, there…in the corner of her mouth…

JOSEPH

What?

HUGH

Let's put the lid back on.

JOSEPH

But, the mortar? Here…I'll scrape off a bit of it.

HUGH

Quickly, now.
(WOODEN LID SLIDES, MUSIC, CHURCH BELL TOLLS, DISTANT DOGS HOWL)

JOSEPH

The tomb is in its new place, but, It looks like it will be a few more days before we can put the heavy slab back on it. The men aren't co-operating. Listen to those dogs...do you think...?

HUGH

The mist is up again surrounding the church...I wouldn't be surprised if...

(WOLF HOWL)

Yes...there it goes again!

JOSEPH

It's the beast! I see it. Oh, if only I had a rifle...there it goes off into the night...Reverend, we should warn the villagers, no?

HUGH

Joseph, as you said...that thing is no dog. If the situation is as I believe it to be, we take our lives in our hands when we venture out into the night to waylay the...

JOSEPH

Why not say it? You believe that thing is a *vampire*, no? It's that body in the tomb, isn't that what you think? Or, her *familiar*, as you call it?

HUGH

Yes. It is, but...it's not yet come to its full strength, thank Heaven! After the starvation of nearly two centuries...at present it can only maraud as a wolf, apparently. But, in a day or two, when full power returns, that dreadful woman in new strength and beauty will be able to leave her refuge. Then, it would not be merely sheep that will satisfy her disgusting lust for blood, but, victims that would yield their life-blood without a murmur to her caressing touch...victims that, dying of her foul embrace, themselves, must become vampires in their turn to prey on others.

JOSEPH

As much as I want to believe you, Reverend...*vampires?* In this day and age? This is *1910*, not the Dark Ages.

HUGH

That little piece of mortar you gave me? I read today in an old book…that, such mortar contains a portion of the Sacred Host, and who holds it, humbly and firmly believing in its virtue, may pass safely through such an ordeal as I intend to submit myself.

JOSEPH

Well, I'll say this…if you're going to investigate further into this mystery…count me in.

(MUSIC, DISTANT CHURCH BELL TOLLS, NIGHT SOUNDS, OWL, DISTANT DOG BARKS)

HUGH

Joseph, I saw it leave just before eleven. It's on the prowl now.

JOSEPH

This fog is as dense as pea soup. And, there's an odor about it…rank and moldy.

HUGH

Like the stench of that tomb when it was opened? If we hide behind that yew tree, we'll have a good view of the entrance to the cemetery.

(DISTANT DOGS HOWL)

JOSEPH

There they go again.

HUGH

(Whispers) And…here *it* comes again! Look…

JOSEPH

(Whispers) I see it! Let's go after it…

HUGH

Hold on!

JOSEPH

It's a grey wolf, alright. It's stopped. It's turning toward us. It's snarling, Reverend. Do you think it knows we're here? Oh, its eyes are burning like fire.

HUGH

Yes, and its jaws are dripping with blood.
                    (LONG HOWL, DISTANT DOGS HOWL)

It's calling to them...the dogs in the village.

JOSEPH

It's turning away...running off into the fog...we're going to lose it!

HUGH

Leave it go, Joseph.

JOSEPH

What is going on here? I can't believe it.

HUGH

Look...here and here...on the stone path...where the beast had stopped...drops of fresh blood.

JOSEPH

If all this is true, Reverend...if this is really happening...how can this unholy Devil exist in the sacred precincts of a church? How can that be?

HUGH

God helps those who help themselves, and by His help and the light of my knowledge we must fight this battle for Him and the poor lost soul within. This battle has just begun.
                                              (MUSIC)

JOSEPH

Well, the workmen from the village are still refusing to come here. I don't know what to do. Some of them have *seen* the devil dog coming out of the mist. They're up all night watching their flock, they sleep all day.

HUGH

That didn't stop it from killing last night. One of the farmers, Martin Berger, found the beast standing over a fresh carcass. He tried to drive it off, but, its size and fierceness so alarmed him that he ran for his gun. When he returned, the animal was gone, though he found that *three* more sheep from his flock were dead and torn.

JOSEPH

If you're right, how much longer before this monster turns to killing people?

HUGH

We must put an end to it, one way or another.

JOSEPH

I hope your solution to the problem works, Reverend.

HUGH

I have prepared everything according to the books I've read...the sharp knives, the pointed stake, fresh garlic, and the wild dog-roses. We are to pierce the vampire through the heart with a stake. Then, standing within a circle of the garlic and flowers which repels the dark spirits, I must read the burial service over the poor clay at last released from its doom. Thus, shall the vampire cease to be, and a lost soul put to rest. But, unfortunately...all this must be done after sunset when the creature is awake.

(DISTANT CHURCH BELL TOLLS)

JOSEPH

She's gone now, I suppose.

HUGH

Yes. The tomb is empty. But, we'll be here when she returns and...I hope she cannot see us if we hide here behind the pulpit. We should have a good view from here. The full moon is out and we can see her clearly returning through the cemetery.

JOSEPH

Odd. I did not notice any fog, tonight...and the village dogs have been silent.

HUGH

Perhaps, she no longer needs to change into a wolf...or, to hide in the fog.   That makes her all the more dangerous. She's out hunting as herself, tonight.

JOSEPH

Hunting? Good God...hunting? You mean...*human beings?*
(MUSIC. CHURCH BELL TOLLS)

It's been hours, Reverend. Perhaps, she won't be returning to
her crypt, after all. Reverend? What are you staring at?

HUGH

See? There's a light mist out there...swirling about...sparkling,
curling...

JOSEPH

It's taking shape. It's *her!* Countess Sarah...

HUGH

(Whispers) She still looks thin and haggard...her face deadly
white...but, those lips on that pale skin...so dark and black
under the moonlight...

JOSEPH

(Whispers) Her eyes...look at her *eyes!* They're orange...fiery.
Here she comes into the church...staggering down the aisle...

HUGH

Still weak from years of being trapped in that tomb. But, make
no mistake...the vampire has a fearful strength not her
own...and like a snake, she can draw her victim willingly to his
own destruction. Be careful, Joseph, stay within the garlic
circle. She won't cross it.

JOSEPH

How can you be sure?   Because, you read that in an old book?
Look at me...I'm shaking like a leaf in a storm.

HUGH

Keep strong. I must pray now.

JOSEPH

Yes, you pray, Reverend. Look...she's going straight to her
tomb. Ah, but, the dog-rose flowers...the garlic...you're right,
she can't cross the line.
(WIND GUSTS, TENSE

MUSIC BUILDS)

Oh no...she's getting angry. Look at her face! Such hate...
she's *smiling* now! She sees us...coming this way...arms
outstretched...

HUGH
Stay within the circle, Joseph...and don't look into her eyes.

JOSEPH
She's licking her lips...

(ECHOING FEMALE VOICE MUFFLED,
PLEASANT, MUTTERING)

What is she saying? I don't understand...

HUGH
Resist it, Joseph! You must...

SARAH (ECHO)
Come! *Come!* I give sleep and peace...sleep and peace...sleep
and peace.

JOSEPH
She's close...so close...

HUGH
Don't listen to her! She can't cross the sacred circle....come
back here!

JOSEPH
No! Let go of me! I *must* go to her! She's so beautiful...

HUGH
Joseph! In the name of all that you hold sacred, be a man!
Hold fast! Wake up, Joseph!

JOSEPH
Where am I?

(SARAH SHRIEKS)

HUGH

Back! Back to your unholy tomb! No longer shall you molest the suffering world! Your end is near.

(SARAH HISSES)

Joseph! Are you alright?

(DISTANT COCK CROWS)

JOSEPH

Yes...I think so.

HUGH

She's gone back into her tomb. Look, the first rays of the sun...Now, will you dare the last terrible act and rid the world forever of this horror?

JOSEPH

By God, I will. Tell me what to do.

HUGH

Help me to lift her out of her tomb. She can harm us no more. Go ahead...she can't hurt you now. That's it...lay her out right down here on the floor. Very good. Why don't you sit and rest? This next part will take a while. Now, I will read the Burial Service over the poor body, and release this living hell that holds her. "Heavenly Father..."

(MUSIC, HAMMERING STAKE, SARAH SCREAMS)

JOSEPH

Is it over yet, Reverend?

HUGH

Yes. Although, for a moment there...the way the body writhed and kicked convulsively, the way she screamed...but, yes, it's over. Come, help me lift the poor body back into its resting place. Come, see...her face is no longer filled with hate....she's at peace now.

JOSEPH

The sharp teeth are gone. She is...*was*... a beautiful woman. *Aaaahhh!* What's happening?

HUGH

She's turned to dust. After all, Joseph, she's almost three hundred years old.

(GUST OF WIND)

JOSEPH

The wind...it's blown the dust away...Good riddens, I say.

HUGH

Let's hope it's all over. Come, we must clean up, now, put everything in order.

(MUSIC)

JOSEPH

It's a beautiful summer's day, hey, Reverend? Since it's been a week and nothing's happened to the local livestock...some of the villagers have returned to work. I must say, they were surprised to see that the body within the tomb has disappeared. I told them that it is a natural result of opening up such an old crypt and exposing it to the air. I don't know if they've accepted that as a satisfactory answer, but, in any case, *The Sarah Tomb* has been sealed up, once again. Why so gloomy, Reverend?

HUGH

Oh? Well...It appears that the child of one of the villagers strayed from home the night of...*you know*...and was found asleep in the field beyond the cemetery. She was very pale and quite exhausted. And...there were two small marks on her throat, which have since disappeared.

JOSEPH

What does this mean?

HUGH

Now that our vampire is no more, there is no further danger either to that child or any other.

JOSEPH

Are you sure about that?

HUGH

According to the book...It is only those who die of the
vampire's embrace that become vampires at death in their turn.

JOSEPH

According to the book?   But, what if the book is *wrong?*   What
if...?

HUGH

I don't know...I just don't know.

(MUSIC)

THE WAXWORK
By Dan Bianchi
From A Story By A.M. Burrage

Cast – 3m
Length – 23 min
Synopsis – A man spends the night in a wax museum

MARRINER
Where do you want this chair, sir? Just here? Then you can talk to Jack The Ripper, when you get tired of doing nothing. Or, there's old Robespierre in the guillotine.

HEWSON
I won't be talking to anyone, Mr. Marriner.

MARRINER
Why? They're just like real people.

HEWSON
They are *not* real. They are wax figures.

MARRINER
We've got Bluebeard standing in the shadows. Next to him is the Axe Man of New Orleans. But, as for Sweeney Todd over there…the demon barber…used to sit his victims in his barber chair and while giving them a shave…with them sitting there helpless and him with his razor…quick as a wink, he'd cut their throats. They say he murdered hundreds that way.

HEWSON
Yes, I know, Mr. Marriner.

MARRINER
Well, I'm just warning you, watch out for him. He's a live one.

HEWSON
Oh, really?

MARRINER
He usually likes to have someone to talk to. Just tell me where

to put it, sir. The chair...

HEWSON
Put the chair right there in the middle of the floor, thank you.

MARRINER
Well, if that will be all? Goodnight, sir. I'm on the floor above if you want me. Don't let any of these figures come up behind you and put their cold hands round your throat.

HEWSON
I won't.

MARRINER
And, watch out for Sweeney. He's...well, just watch out for him.

HEWSON
That'll be all tonight, Mr. Marriner. See you in the morning. Good night.
                                    (DOOR CLOSE, CLOCK STRIKES)

"Oh, is it that time already? Six, seven hours to go. That's not so bad. Well, I won't be facing you all that time, Mr. Sweeney Todd. For some reason, I'd rather not look in your direction. Oh, my aching bones...well, we've got a long night ahead of us. Very quiet tonight, isn't it? Can't even hear the usual noise from the street. No, not a sound. I feel I'm on the floor of the sea. Oh, that sounds poetic. I must remember to put that into my story. Is someone watching me? Ah...Mr.Todd again. I can feel his dark eyes staring at me. Insistent fellow, isn't he? But...If I turn round now, it only shows that I'm afraid. Or is it...just because you are afraid, that you can't turn round and look?
                                    (CHAIR SCRAPES FLOOR)

"Well...I'll turn my chair just a bit. There now. I'm looking. Satisfied? You know, it could be that there's a stronger light on you, Sweeney Todd, stronger than the rest. That's why you stand out. Although, I must say...that face is expertly made. A real master of wax made you. But, those eyes...they're not wax. They're glistening. Wet. So, *real.* Fool! He's only waxwork. Only a waxwork. Same as the others. Only waxworks. But...waxworks don't move. Oh, there look! I could have sworn...did one actually move? No, you fool. Wait...The Ripper...he's standing a little differently. I'm sure of it. And, Bluebeard...wasn't he turned a little more to the left? You know what? It's the way your chair is turned around... you're seeing things from a different angle. That's it. I should jot down some notes...Let see ...'Everything quiet. Feel I'm on the floor of the sea. Sweeney Todd trying to send me to sleep with his eyes. Figures seem to move when you're not watching.' That should do it for tonight. I suppose. Oh (Yawns) Getting late. You're not actually going to sleep, are you? Oh, be quiet. That's fear talking. Hold on...is Sweeney Todd moving again when I look away? I see what's happening. He just waits for me to take my eyes off him, *then* , he makes his move. That's what they *all* do. I know it! It's too much! I have to get up. Get out of here. I'm not staying all night with a lot of murderers, moving about when I'm not looking! Oh, sit down, sit down. Stop being so jumpy. Only waxworks, they're only...Alright, then, so why am I so afraid? Either *that,* or someone *is* playing tricks on me. The Ripper's *eyes!* They're beckoning me to look over to him, but...*Aha!* Nearly caught you that time, Mr.Todd! Be careful, I'm *warning* you... and all you others. If I do catch you moving, I'm going to break your arms and legs off. Do you hear?

(CLOCK STRIKES)

"Anyway, it's only been an hour, but, I can leave now. I've got a lot to write about. A good story ... *ten* good stories! My editor isn't going to know how long I stayed here. Who cares? But, Mr. Marriner is going to laugh if he sees me leaving so early. And, then, there's the money I paid him to let me spend the night. I don't want to lose that. But , this is too hard. It's bad enough the waxworks move behind my back, but, it's even worse that they can breathe. *Listen!* Do you hear them breathing? Or, is that my breathing? Or, was it just *his* breathing, seeming to come from far away? You know what they're doing, don't you? They're like children in a classroom ...turn your back for a second and they're whispering and laughing and playing pranks. There you go again. You must think about other things. Who are you? I'm Raymond Hewson. I live and breathe. These figures round me aren't living. They can't move and speak as I can. They're only made of wax. They just stand there for old ladies and little boys to look at. There …doesn't that make you feel better? No, Sweeney Todd is still staring at me. Alright, sir, you want to gawk at me…I'll stare right back at you! Face to face. See how *you* like it. Ripper! You moved, you dirty swine! Yes you did. I saw you! Okay, alright, okay…just sit here now…try to stop shaking. Oh, Jesus, Mary and Joseph…Sweeney Todd…he's moving now right in front of me…getting down off his stand and…sitting right in front of me.   Smiling at me…"

SWEENEY

Good evening. I did not know that I was going to have a friend here tonight. Then, I heard you and Marriner talking. You cannot move or speak now until I tell you. But, you can hear me, quite easily, I know. Something tells me that you are … let's say, a little *afraid* of me. Make no mistake, sir. I am not one of these poor dead figures suddenly turned into a living thing. Oh no. I *am* Sweeney Todd in person. I must sit awhile. I *am* sorry, but, my arms and legs are quite tired. I don't want to take up your time with my uninteresting story. I can just say that some unusual happenings brought me to this place. I was near this building this evening, when I saw a policeman looking at me, too closely. I thought, perhaps, he wanted to ask me some difficult questions, so, I quickly came in here with all the other visitors. Then, I had a very good idea. When the wax museum was closing, I stayed behind…. I undressed that figure of me, put on its coat and quickly put the figure at the back of the room, where nobody could see it. Then, I took its place here on the stand.   I must say that I had a very tiring evening. But, luckily the people didn't watch me all the time. I could breathe sometimes and move my arms and legs a little.

HEWSON

But, but…but…

SWEENEY

What Marriner said about me was not very nice, you know. However, he was right about one thing… I am not dead. It's important that the world thinks I am. What he said about my doings is mostly right, too. Most people, you know, collect something or other. Some collect books, some collect money, others collect pictures or train tickets. And me? I collect throats.

HEWSON

Throats?

SWEENEY

I'm happy you came tonight. You mustn't think that I don't want you here. It was difficult for me to do any interesting *collecting* over the last few months. So, now, I'm happy to go back to my usual work. I'm sorry to see that your throat is a little thin, sir. Perhaps, that is not a nice thing to say. But, I like men with big throats best. Big, thick, red throats...

HEWSON

What do you have there under your coat?

SWEENEY

This? This is a little French razor. Perhaps, you know them. They do not cut very far *into* the throat, but, they cut very *cleanly*, I find. In just a minute, I am going to show you how well they cut. But, first, I must ask the question that I always ask... is the razor to your liking, sir?

HEWSON

"Oh, Sweet Jesus...he's coming at me now. Slowly, like a cat stalking a bird. My feet, I can't move. I'm paralyzed."

SWEENEY

Please be so good as to put your head back a little. Thank you. And, now, a little more. Just a little more. Ah, thank you! That's right... Thank you... Thank you...

(MUSIC)

MARRINER

That's the way I found him, Officer...I came in this morning to open up and...I checked all the waxworks, to see if they need dusting....and, then, I look and see him there in the center of the room...just sitting there with his head far back in his armchair. Dead. Stone cold dead. As if he's getting a shave. But, the funny thing is, in his hand...he's holding a razor, you see? It comes from the Sweeney Todd exhibit cross the room.

There's not a mark on him, as you can see. Why is he holding it, I wonder? I shouldn't have let him in, I know, but, he was so insistent on spending the night among the figures. I don't know why. They're only waxworks. It's not as if they're *real* people, you know?

THE GREAT GOD PAN
By Dan Bianchi
From A Story by Arthur Machen

Cast – 2m
Length – 30 min
Synopsis – A man discovers the mystery behind a strange woman

VILLIERS

So, as I was saying, this girl, Helen…at the age of eleven was adopted by a farmer and his family. No one knew her, her origin or her real name. She was found abandoned by the roadside. Well, everyone said the same thing about her…she was very beautiful, but, had a certain weirdness about her.

CLARKE

A certain *weirdness?*

VILLIERS

Well, she'd run off and stay in the woods for hours, a whole day at a time. Once, the farmer's young son followed her into the woods and returned in utter shock at what he had seen.

CLARKE

What did he see?

VILLIERS

He said that the girl had met with a strange man…a naked man covered in hair…with hind legs like that of an animal. It took some time for the boy to calm down. He was hysterical.

CLARKE

What about the girl?

VILLIERS

When they questioned Helen, she simply laughed it off. Well, time passed and…a few years go by and for some reason, the boy, now in his teens… was brought to the city for some health problem and…upon entering a building…he suddenly broke out in wild screams, pointing to something on the façade of the building.

CLARKE

Well, what was it?

VILLIERS

Well, you see, on this particular building, the architect had thought to add some sculptural elements over each window …the head of a horned satyr.

CLARKE

You mean, like a *gargoyle?*

VILLIERS

Yes. Smiling devilishly. The boy saw this and grew hysterical again claiming that… *that's* what he had seen in the woods that day with Helen.

CLARKE

Amazing.

VILLIERS

Now, about that time, back in the farmer's village…a girl named Rachel had befriended Helen…they were older now…well, she had joined Helen in her excursions into the woods. One day, she came home, quite upset, crying…"Mother! Why did you let me go with Helen into the woods?" Thereupon, she told her mother a horrifying story…God knows what…and when Rachel's parents went to seek out Helen…they found her in an open field…far off enough that they could barely see a figure accompanying her.

CLARKE

A figure?

VILLIERS

Yes, a figure. It was *not* a man…a human being…of that they were certain. But, a few moments later…Helen was gone. Disappeared.

CLARKE

You mean, she didn't return to her home at the farm?

VILLIERS

No. She was *gone*. No one had any idea of where she'd gone off to. Some thought she'd been kidnapped.

CLARKE

Amazing.

VILLIERS

No, *this* is what is amazing. Ten more years go by. I was in Boston where I came across an old school mate of ours... remember Charles Herbert?

CLARKE

Charles Herbert? *Charles Herbert!* Yes!

VILLIERS

Well, I must say, he was in terrible shape. Appeared to me to be a street beggar. He approached me with his hand out. In fact, *he* was the one who had recognized me.

CLARKE

A beggar? Hadn't he inherited a fortune?

VILLIERS

All gone. He had married a woman, you see. A beautiful girl with a mysterious background. Her name was Helen.

CLARKE

Helen? *No!* You mean...?

VILLIERS

Now, if you remember, Charles Herbert was a religious fellow. Never missed church on Sunday. Well, he said that his bride had completely corrupted him. He wound up doing things, *vile* things, he wouldn't even reveal to me. He told me that he had *seen* things with her...

CLARKE

Things? What kind of *things?*

VILLIERS

Incredible horrors that had led him to madness and ruination.

Utter dissolution of mind and spirit. And, of course, she had taken all of his money and disappeared, as well. The poor man had sunk lower and lower until...well, I gave him a meal and some money, but...

CLARKE

Helen...

VILLIERS

She told him that her name was Helen Vaughn, but, even Herbert doubted that was her real name. He said that...

CLARKE

What?

VILLIERS

He said that...only *human beings* have names. Then, he said good by and promised to look me up again if he needed help.

CLARKE

That *is* a strange story. I wonder what he had experienced with this Helen that drove him to such a state? And, is *that* Helen the same as the young orphan girl you spoke of? How do we know?

VILLIERS

Well, his story bothered me...enough that I had to delve into it a bit further. I wanted to find out more about the Herberts. So, I drove around to where he had lived and started asking questions in the local taverns and...turns out his neighbors were astonished that I had not heard about the *Paul Street case* which was a sensation in the press just three years earlier.

CLARKE

The Paul Street case...? Doesn't ring a bell.

VILLIERS

A man...a well-to-do sort, a banker...was found dead in the alley behind 33 Paul Street...the Herberts' home. He was bruised a bit, as if thrown down the steps at the back of the house. But, that was the only sign of violence upon the man.

                    CLARKE
A robbery?

                    VILLIERS
No. He had on him his wallet and a valuable watch.

                    CLARKE
How did he die?

                    VILLIERS
The police immediately assumed he'd been shoved out the
door down the steps. But, the medical examiner had a hard
time finding out the real cause of death. They *say*, the look on
the corpse's face...

                    CLARKE
What?

                    VILLIERS
Sheer terror. As if he had died by fright. So goes the rumor.
The Herberts were questioned, but, denied knowing anything
about the incident. But, the general consensus was that they
had *something* to do with it. From what I had gathered...they
weren't well liked in that neighborhood. The people looked on
them as being...*odd.*

                    CLARKE
I see. And, the man died of fright, you say?

                    VILLIERS
Well, heart attack. The Herberts couldn't very well be
suspected of frightening a man to death, so, that was that.
Although, who knows what they were up to? Charles did say
they were into all manners of things, *evil* things.

                    CLARKE
Does that mean...*satanic* things?

                    VILLIERS
Who knows? That wife of his...The neighbors I questioned
...they all said the same thing about Helen...a strikingly
beautiful woman, but, also the most repulsive being they had

ever set eyes on.

CLARKE

Imagine that.

VILLIERS

And, another thing...people wondered what that dead man was doing there? This was at a time when the Herberts had come down in class. Paul Street is in the run-down section of town, you know? The victim, well, he was a millionaire banker.

CLARKE

I wonder what really killed him? Had he *seen* something so terrifying that...it cut short his life? How long did the Herberts stay at that house?

VILLIERS

The landlord said they had left shortly after the incident.

CLARKE

Landlord? You went to the house itself?

VILLIERS

Oh yes. A hovel is more like it. Still dusty and dirty and desolate. I can't describe it, but...well, if you believe in such things...there's no doubt that the house has a sense of foreboding about it. Stuffy, a heaviness I could feel as soon as I entered it. I walked into the front room and...I *swear*, Clarke, I nearly fainted. My limbs were suddenly trembling. My heart beating. I felt it was overwhelming. Beating me down. There were old newspapers scattered about and then I found this ...this curious drawing. Well, I barely got out and staggered home and was in bed for a week. The doctor called it exhaustion.

CLARKE

That's terrible. I didn't know...

VILLIERS

Yes, well. While I was recuperating, I read in the paper that our friend Charles Herbert had died.

CLARKE

Oh?

VILLIERS

Yes. *Starved* to death.

CLARKE

Starved to death?

VILLIERS

If it were any other poor wretch, it would have gone unnoticed. But, since he had come from a wealthy family at one time, the paper gave him a short article.

CLARKE

Such a tragedy. On the other hand, James, it sounds as if he had brought it all upon himself. Do you think there's any mystery to *his* death, as well?

VILLIERS

It all has to do with that woman whom he married, I'm sure of it. *She* is the mystery.

CLARKE

And, what about that house of theirs? Hey, and what about that drawing you found?

VILLIERS

Oh yes, here it is. It's a sketch of a woman's head. It's drawn quite well.

CLARKE

Who is she?

VILLIERS

Look at the back of it. See what it says?

CLARKE

Helen.

VILLIERS

That was enough for me.

CLARKE

That's a strange story alright, James. But, if you want *my* advice, toss that drawing into the fireplace and blot the story out of your mind. Don't give it another thought.

VILLIERS

But, my experience in that house...in that room...

CLARKE

You see? You're driving yourself to madness over all of this nonsense. It's affecting your health, your mind.

VILLIERS

That house...It was as if I were inhaling some deadly fume, which seemed to penetrate to every nerve and bone and sinew of my body. I felt racked from head to foot, my eyes began to grow dim... it was like standing at the entrance of death.

CLARKE

Well, now...*now,* you're getting yourself *too* involved to the point of...

VILLIERS

Oh, I'm involved alright. More than you may guess. But, first... Look...I want to show you something. A print, a picture in a book I have here somewhere...yes, here. It's in here...here it is. Take a look.

CLARKE

Ah. Alright. Well, that's rather...disturbing...

VILLIERS

It's a painting...of Walpurgis Night.

CLARKE

What's that?

VILLIERS

May 1st. It's when all sorts of strange, monstrous things celebrate evil.

CLARKE

I thought that was on Halloween.

VILLIERS

There, what do you see? Those are figures of *fauns* and horned *satyrs* dancing about, no? Not unlike the *thing* that boy claimed he had seen frolicking with Helen in the woods…and like that statue he had seen on the building.

CLARKE

Yes. You're right.

VILLIERS

And, another thing…in the center there…that naked woman. Take a good look at her face.

CLARKE

Her face? That's weird. It looks like the drawing you have. No…it can't be her.   The weird Mrs. Herbert? *Helen?* It's a coincidence. Although, it's the same pose, the same lighting and shading. I suppose this little sketch was used in the painting…by, let's see, Henry Meyrick. Never heard of him.

VILLIERS

Take a look at that sketch again. What do you see, there, down left?

CLARKE

It's initialed…H.M. Henry Meyrick! Well, that settles *that.* Maybe, *he* knows where Helen is.

VILLIERS

Well, if he was alive, he could tell us.   Henry Meyrick died three years ago. *Suicide.* Don't you see?

CLARKE

What?

VILLIERS

He was probably yet another victim of Helen!

CLARKE

You really think Helen was connected to this artist, Meyrick?

VILLIERS

Well, *he* killed himself. Do you want to know how? He *starved* himself to death.

CLARKE

No!

VILLIERS

He's not the only one. Here's a newspaper clipping…I've been collecting them, you see…here. Just weeks ago, a Lord Argentine had also taken his life…just after he was seen dining with a beautiful woman that night. He then went home and hanged himself.

CLARKE

And, you think this woman he dined with was Helen?

VILLIERS

Maybe. Maybe not. But, I'm sure she was connected in some way.

CLARKE

Well, he didn't starve himself.

VILLIERS

Within the following three weeks… there were three more gentlemen, all wealthy men, who had also taken their own lives. The police are still dumbfounded, of course. There is no obvious motive, no suicide note in any case.

CLARKE

Coincidences? Surely, we can't attribute these suicides to the woman known as Helen Vaughn.

VILLIERS

Oh, by then, she was no longer calling herself Helen Vaughn.

CLARKE

What?

VILLIERS

By this time, her name was *Mrs .Beaumont*. Apparently, she'd taken the town by storm. They said she was a remarkable woman. Striking, in every way. Quite a lot of men flocked around her wherever she went.

CLARKE

If what you say is true...

VILLIERS

But, *it is!* Here...here's a testimony from a witness who saw one of her victims on the night of his death. He said he had run into him on the street and the man's face...his eyes glared at him "as if a lost soul on his way to Hell. It was a *devil's* face." Read it yourself. An hour later the victim was dead. Threw himself off the Brooklyn Bridge.

CLARKE

This is too much. What can it mean?

VILLIERS

There's something terrible going on here, Clarke. All you have to do is to take one look at that woman and...

CLARKE

James...have you seen this Mrs. Beaumont, or, Mrs. Herbert, or, whomever she is?

VILLIERS

I have. Well, I told you...I got involved in all this and...I've been investigating and...I first saw her, Clarke...downtown.

CLARKE

First saw her?

VILLIERS

I saw her entering a house in one of the most miserable and disreputable streets in the city.

CLARKE

How did you find her?

VILLIERS

I've been in some dangerous places searching for that woman. I had to deal with people you wouldn't be caught dead with. Of course, if I had just gone to her house on Bleecker Street and accused Mrs.Beaumont of all this...well, she'd deny it and that would be that. She'd laugh me off...as she had done to that boy when they were children. I can't go to the police. As you say, where is the evidence? They'd think I'm mad. Do *you* think I'm mad?

CLARKE

Me? Well, the story is rather...

VILLIERS

No, I had to catch this she-devil at work, so to speak. What do you think I found? In that slum...some five or six years ago, a woman named *Miss Renay* rented a room on Jay Street. She was young, beautiful, fresh, as if she had come from the country. But, according to one of her neighbors, who is a prostitute...there were *things* that went on in Miss Renay's apartment that even *she* couldn't bring herself to tell me. She alluded to strange sounds and chants and...screams of sexual ecstasy.

CLARKE

Orgies?

VILLIERS

I wanted to know more.

CLARKE

I don't blame you.

VILLIERS

I even offered to *pay* her for more details.

CLARKE

Good Lord...

VILLIERS

So, Miss Renay lived there on Jay Street for about six months and then vanished. I believe that she took up with the artist Meyrick about then. Posing for him and God knows what else. Perhaps...well, if there really *was* something bizarre about this woman....I suppose she led him into some underworld that...I know this sounds really far-fetched, but....this picture of his... the things in this picture... perhaps, it wasn't *all* conjured up from an artist's imagination.

CLARKE

What are you saying, James?

VILLIERS

I don't know.

CLARKE

Next, you'll be accusing her of witchcraft and wanting to burn her at the stake! This is 1892, *not* 1692, remember?

VILLIERS

So, then, she disappeared again and the people on Jay Street saw nothing of her until a few months ago. I was informed that she had rented a room again on the same block and visited it two or three times a week and always at ten in the morning. So, I kept watch.

CLARKE

You didn't!

VILLIERS

Oh yes. Every morning at ten...until, *one day*...she came walking down the street. And, she glanced over at me across the street and...it's a look I'll never forget. I knew right then and there. That woman, Miss Renay...*she's* the one. Mrs. Herbert. Mrs. Beaumont. Helen Vaughn. Whatever. God knows how many other names she's had over the years.

CLARKE

So, what happened?

VILLIERS

So, she went into the house and I kept watch until four o'clock when she came out, and, then, I followed her. It was a long chase, and I had to be very careful to keep a long way in the background, and yet not lose sight of the woman. She took me down to the Battery, and then up to Canal Street and then, Houston Street. Then, she arrived at Bleecker Street....where she, as Mrs. Beaumont, was living. I waited at the corner, keeping my eye on her all the time, and I took particular care to note the house at which she stopped. A minute later, an empty carriage came round and stopped in front of the house. Mrs. Herbert was going out for a drive.

CLARKE

Did she know you had followed her?

VILLIERS

It's possible.

CLARKE

So...what now?

VILLIERS

Well, I came to the conclusion that...I should visit Mrs. Beaumont...or, Miss Renay.

CLARKE

But, it would be dangerous, James. All those men who have died mysterious deaths...it's creepy.

VILLIERS

Ah, so you *admit* that I was dealing with something completely out of the ordinary here?

CLARKE

There is the hint of the supernatural, I'll admit.

VILLIERS

I have something else to show you. Here...

CLARKE

A manuscript?

VILLIERS

This is the sworn testimony of a man who had fallen under her spell as Mrs. Beaumont and, yet, barely escaped with his life. As it is, his doctors predict that he has not long for this world. He's a wreck of a man. His nerves completely shattered. He says...he has *seen*...the Great God Pan.

CLARKE

Pan?

VILLIERS

The Greek god of the woods, of sexuality and fertility. The god of spring time. He was a *satyr*...one of those half man-half creature things that run around the woods. Playing his pipes. He was also the god of theatrical criticism.

CLARKE

Well, that's a kick in the head. A beastly drama critic, as well, huh? That's even *worse* than being a satyr. A *satyr?* Seems I've heard that word a few times tonight.

VILLIERS

Sound familiar? Well, the ancient Greeks believed...this world around us...All the scenery out there? Or, even now, you see me standing right here in front of you, right? It's all unreal. Like a veil hiding the real world behind it. They believed that the veil can be lifted and when it is...they called it *seeing the Great God Pan.*

CLARKE

Seeing the Great God Pan. But, is that good... or bad?

VILLIERS

It may start out as good...that's how it gets one hooked...but, I think it leads to horror beyond imagination. And, Mrs. Beaumont...Helen...she was at the root of this horror. I know that for certain now.

CLARKE

All the more reason why you shouldn't ever meet her face to face, James. You know too much about her. You might not get out alive.

VILLIERS

Too late, my friend.

CLARKE

What? What do you mean? What's that you have there?
Rope?

VILLIERS

It is the best hempen cord, just as it used to be made for the
old trade. That's what the old man who sold it to me told me.
Not an inch of jute from end to end.

CLARKE

Are you crazy? You can't have blood on your hands. My *God!*
You can't mean this, James...you will make yourself a
hangman?

VILLIERS

I had no choice...

CLARKE

Had no choice? What do you mean...*had no choice?* What are
you talking about?

VILLIERS

I locked the door behind me and gave her fifteen minutes to
decide...

CLARKE

You *went* there? You *saw* her?

VILLIERS

I left Helen Vaughan alone with this cord in a locked room for
fifteen minutes. If she didn't hang herself, I'd reveal everything
to the world.

CLARKE

I can't listen to this! This is...crazy, James! *Crazy!* What
you're saying... it's preposterous and I won't be part of it.

VILLIERS

She's gone, Clarke.

CLARKE

What? She fled again? From a locked room?

VILLIERS

No. I mean, she's dead. Quite dead.

CLARKE

You mean...

VILLIERS

When I re-entered the room...though horror and revolting nausea rose up within me, and an odor of corruption choked my breath, I remained firm. I then saw something lying on the bed, lying there black like ink, transforming before my eyes.

(WEIRD MUSIC)

The skin, and the flesh, and the muscles, and the bones, and the firm structure of the human body began to melt and dissolve. I could not believe what I saw. There was some internal force causing the dissolution and change.

CLARKE

This is madness, James.

VILLIERS

All the work by which man had been made repeated itself before my eyes. I saw the form waver from sex to sex, dividing itself *from* itself, and, then, again, reunited. Then, I saw the body descend to that of a beast... backwards in evolution down to the depths where it had begun. To the beginning of life itself. The light within the room had turned to utter blackness. Objects appeared before my eyes. I don't know how. I watched, and, at last, I saw nothing but a substance that looked like jelly. In a flash, I saw a form which I cannot describe. But, the symbol of this form may be seen in ancient sculptures, and in paintings, too foul to be spoken of... as a horrible and unspeakable shape, neither man nor beast...then, it changed into human form and finally, death.

(SILENCE)

CLARKE

This...is insanity. You're not in your right mind, my friend. No, no...I can't believe any of this. *I can't.* Oh, this is all...I mean, what does it all *mean?* Who is...*was...* this woman? Where did she come from? What does it all have to do with the *Great God Pan?* And, why have *you* become so obsessed with this? What's it got to do with you, James?

VILLIERS

Now, Clarke...I will tell you. It's a part of the story I neglected to tell you until now, because...well, I had blocked it out of my mind all these years. Until recently, when all of *this* resurrected my past. Especially, reading that man's testimony where he mentioned the Great God Pan. You see, many years ago, while in college...I had worked for a Professor Raymond. I helped him to carry out his experiments upon the human brain...the mind, itself. He was so sure that he could reach some other world within *our* world if a certain unused portion of the brain might be finally utilized. He called it *transcendental medicine.* Well, as you can imagine, the rest of his colleagues mocked his efforts, called him a quack, but, he continued on his own. With *me* at his side. Eventually, Raymond was convinced he had finally found the answer to his theory and he insisted that we find a human subject upon which to experiment. We found her. Her name was Mary. A young girl who willingly allowed him to carry out his dream. Well, his dream involved injecting her with a solution and then carrying out brain surgery and...

CLARKE

And?

VILLIERS

When the poor girl awakened...the look on her face...her head rolling from side to side...she screamed in terror.

(BLOODY SCREAM ECHOES)

I can still hear her now. She became a hopeless idiot for the rest of her life.

CLARKE

So, the operation failed.

VILLIERS

Not completely, according to Professor Raymond. No, he said that Mary had crossed over to the *other* side, alright, beyond the veil...she had seen things no other human was meant to see...she had seen the *Great God Pan.*

CLARKE

Oh dear Lord...

VILLIERS

Yes, I remembered those words, that's how he described it. I figured that Professor Raymond, who is still alive, he must know *something* about all this. And, so, last week, I traveled up to Boston to his home and he told me what he knew. When I showed him the portrait and the picture in the book of Helen's face...

CLARKE

What?

VILLIERS

That wasn't Helen. That was *her mother*. That was Mary. The girl he and I had experimented upon.

CLARKE

You didn't recognize her?

VILLIERS

I did...at first. But, I couldn't believe there would be any connection to her. The drawing had Helen's name on the back of it. The face in the painting looked identical, so...I guess she looked just like her mother.

CLARKE

So, *Mary* was Helen's mother...

VILLIERS

She gave birth to her exactly nine months after the night of the experiment.

CLARKE

Oh, really? Exactly nine months after the night of the

experiment?

VILLIERS

Don't look at me like that. It wasn't me. And, it *wasn't* Professor Raymond.

CLARKE

Well, it wasn't the angel Gabriel.

VILLIERS

He told me that Mary never recovered her reason. She died a few days after the child was born. He says, she regained her senses a moment before dying, looked up at him and...

CLARKE

But, then...*who* was the father of Helen?

VILLIERS

Don't you see? Raymond's experiment broke open the door of the house of life, without knowing or caring what might get out *or* enter in. At the same time, he ruined the reason of a human being. It was a foolish experiment based on an absurd theory. That's what I had told him at the time. But, it was not *all* absurdity. Mary crossed over. She saw something. No, she *experienced* something. Something no human eyes should have seen without some sort of repudiation. She had crossed over *through the veil* to see what lurked behind it, something for which we have no name, and while there...somehow, she met the Great God Pan...the god of sexuality and fertility and...

CLARKE

Are you saying...she was *raped* by...this *thing?* How? All the while her physical self...was *lying* on the operating table. How can that be?

VILLIERS

I don't profess to understand it. But, according to Professor Raymond, that's pretty much what happened. That painting by Meyrick...I guess that was his conception of what had happened. I don't know. We'll never know.

CLARKE

Wait. Did you *tell* any of this to Helen while handing her a noose?

VILLIERS

Helen Vaughan did well to bind the cord about her neck and die, though the death was horrible. When I cut her down...she fell to the bed and...the blackened face, the hideous form upon the bed, changing and melting before my eyes from woman to man, from man to beast, and from beast to worse than beast. Professor Raymond told me...when he saw what Mary had given birth to all those years ago...he shuddered. He knew what he had done the moment the child was born. So, he took the orphaned child to raise. He says, that, when Helen was about five years old, he surprised her playing in the yard, not once or twice, but, several times. She was with a playmate... you may guess of what kind. It was for him a constant, an *incarnate* horror, and after a few years he felt he could bear it no more, and he sent Helen Vaughan away. You know now what frightened the boy in the woods. And, the girl Rachel...and all those men driven to madness and suicide. And, now, as far as we know, Helen is with her companions...

_____

OUT OF THE DEPTHS
By Dan Bianchi
From A Story By Robert W. Chambers

Cast – 4m, 1w
Length – 25 min
Synopsis – A dead man returns to set things straight

(CROWDED BAR SOUNDS)

JAMES
Michael! I thought I'd find you here.

MICHAEL
What? Have you been looking for me?

JAMES
Plan to stay in New York for long?

MICHAEL
Not long. Bartender! A martini? Dry, with olives.

JAMES
I thought you had cut that out?

MICHAEL
What? Drinking? Not at all. Not that I can't stop, if I want to. Ah, thank you my good man. Down the hatch. Ah! Nectar of the gods. I'll have another.

JAMES
Maybe, you shouldn't have another?

MICHAEL
Who are you, my mother? This town has gotten on my nerves and I need a good strong tonic to help me wash the blues away. Business is worse than dead... I can't hold on much longer. I need alcohol to drown my sorrows. The world has hammered me to the ropes, and it will be down and out for me unless...

JAMES

Unless you can borrow on your own terms?

MICHAEL

Yes, but I can't. The banks...

JAMES

You are mistaken.

MICHAEL

Oh, am I? Who is going to lend me...?

JAMES

I will.

MICHAEL

You! Don't kid.

JAMES

I'm not.

MICHAEL

Listen, do you know how much I need? Do you know for how long I shall need it?

JAMES

Yes.

MICHAEL

Do you know what the chances are of my making good to you? You! Why, hell, I'd swamp you! You can't afford...

JAMES

I can afford anything...now.

MICHAEL

Have you struck it rich? Won a lottery? A long shot at the Kentucky Derby? What?

JAMES

Don't worry about it. I've got more than I need, more than I want. Here, here's my checkbook. Fill out the sum you need.

Here's a pen.

MICHAEL

Are you crazy?

JAMES

No.

MICHAEL

Is this check going to bounce tomorrow morning?

JAMES

Not at all. Fill it out, pocket it and use it.

MICHAEL

I can't do that. My security is rotten, I tell you...but, I'm not a charity case.

JAMES

Believe me, I don't need it. Take it. I am here, tonight, for this.

MICHAEL

You are here, tonight...to help me?

JAMES

To help you, Michael.

MICHAEL

Why?

JAMES

I've been a lonely man in life. I think you never realized how much your friendship has meant to me. I have nobody...no intimacies. You never understood....you with all your friends ...that I cared more for our casual companionship than for anything in the world.

MICHAEL

Really? Well, I never realized...all this time. I mean, recent times have been rough for me. I don't know which way to turn. You really mean it, James?

JAMES

Yes.

MICHAEL

It's like a dream come true. This can't be happening. I was just about to toss it all in...if you know what I mean? Look at me, shaking...trying to understand what has happened....what you have just done for me. It's got me all emotional. No one's ever done something like this for me before.

(GLASS BREAKS)

Damn! Sorry about that! I'm trembling so...I can't even hold my glass. James! What sort of a man am I to deserve this of you? What can I do...?

JAMES

Keep your nerve, for one thing.

MICHAEL

I will!

JAMES

There's more.

MICHAEL

Just tell me. What will you let me do for you?

JAMES

Well, for one thing, you can stop drinking. Let's go into a side booth. I've got something to tell you.

(MUSIC)

I'll bet you don't remember where we first met?

MICHAEL

Was it...here?

JAMES

You had just come back to town from Canada, and I saw you stroll in and seat yourself at the bar, and, because I was sitting next to you, you asked if you could buy me a drink.

MICHAEL

Yes, I remember.

JAMES

And, I told you I was new in town and you told me some of the great spots to visit and where to stay. You spent time talking to me. Do you remember me talking about a child?

MICHAEL

Child?

JAMES

There was a beautiful child I used to see every day when I'd have my lunch on a bench in Central Park and the child used to be there every day and she'd leave her nanny and talk to me over near the zoo?

MICHAEL

Now that you mention it...yeah, I do remember that...but...?

JAMES

Well, that's why I came here tonight to tell you about her. You see, you're not the only one having bad times.

MICHAEL

But..?

JAMES

Listen! Her parents are dead... she is not yet twenty. She isn't equipped to support herself in life... and she *is* beautiful. What chance has she here in the city, Michael? What chance? And, when I tell you that she is a naive person, and that she reasons only with her heart, answer me...what chance has *she* with a man? For you know men, and so do I, Michael, so do I.

MICHAEL

I don't understand...who is she?

JAMES

The victim of divorced parents...mean, rotten parents who had only cared about themselves. In the end, they have both left her all too early. Left her to fend for herself in the city.

Penniless. Anyway, the dead are no concern of yours. What concerns you is the living. The child, grown to womanhood, is here, advertising for employment...here in New York, asking for a chance. But, what chance has she?

MICHAEL

When did you learn this?

JAMES

I learned it tonight...everything concerning her...tonight...an hour before I ...I met you. That is why I returned.

MICHAEL

What do you want *me* to do?

JAMES

Now, listen to me, pay attention. Listen to every word I say. Do you remember a passing fancy you had this spring for a blue-eyed girl you met every morning on your way downtown?

MICHAEL

What?

JAMES

Do you remember that, as the days went on, little by little, she came to return your glance?   Then, your smile? Then, at last, your greeting? And, do you remember, once....remember, you told me about it in a moment of depression...told me that you were close to infatuation, that, you believed her to be everything sweet and innocent, that, you dared not drift any farther, knowing the chances and knowing the end...bitter unhappiness either way, whether in guilt or innocence...

MICHAEL

I remember, but...that is...it can't be...

JAMES

She is the girl, Michael.

MICHAEL

Not the child you told me of...? The one in Central Park?

JAMES

Yes.

MICHAEL

How…when did you know…?

JAMES

Tonight. I know more than that, Michael. You will learn it later.
Now, ask me again, what it is that you may do?

MICHAEL

Alright…what am I to do?

JAMES

(Pause) It is time for us to go.

MICHAEL

You want us to go out?

JAMES

Yes… we will walk together for a little while…as we did in the
old days, Michael…only a little while, for I must be going back.

MICHAEL

Where are you going? Hey, wait up! I'm coming…
                              (MUSIC, STREET NOISE)

Hold on, James! Where are…where are you going?

JAMES

Don't you know?

MICHAEL

James, why…why are you here with me in this street tonight?
What do you know? *How* do you know? I tell you I…this is
maddening…the tension…I can't endure this…

JAMES

She is enduring it.

MICHAEL

Good God!

JAMES

Yes, God is good.

MICHAEL

Answer me, James, where are we going?

JAMES

To *her*...you know it!

MICHAEL

James! I don't even know where she lives. How did you know about her...me?

JAMES

I didn't know myself until an hour before I met you tonight.

MICHAEL

I had not seen her in weeks...I had not dared to...how could I? My financial situation...I couldn't even speak to her....to ask another human being to trust in me. I've got no future. Then, just at dusk, today...we passed each other, and, before I understood what I had done we were side by side. And, almost instantly...I don't know how...she seemed to sense the ruin before us both...she could see it in my eyes...in my soul! I stood there, trying to smile, while, inside... She *knew* she was losing me. I told her what she wanted to hear. I said I would come to her. She didn't answer. But, in her eyes, James, I *saw* what one sees in the eyes of children, and, it stunned me... What shall I do?

JAMES

Go to her and look again. That is what I have come to ask of you. This is her home here. Third floor. Back apartment. Good-by.

MICHAEL

Where are you going, James? Come back! I don't even know her name!

JAMES

Her name? Linda! Tell her that I remember her there in Central Park by the zoo. Tell her that I have searched for her always, but, that it was only tonight I knew what tomorrow she shall know... and you, Michael, you, too, shall know. Good-by.

MICHAEL

James! Wait! Don't go...

                    (FOOTSTEPS ON SIDEWALK
             RETREAT, MUSIC.RUNNING UPSTAIRS,
              KNOCKING ON DOOR, DOOR OPENS.)

(Pause) Hello...What is it? You're trembling. You don't have to. Everything is going to be alright. Look into my eyes. Look into my eyes, I'm telling you the truth.

                                      (SHE SOBS)

From the very first first moment I saw you...I've loved you!

LINDA

I love you, too.

MICHAEL

Oh, Linda! *Linda!* You see? I know your name!

LINDA

How?

MICHAEL

Everything is going to be so different now. Everything I've ever wanted is right here in my arms. I want to give you everything, the world...see how happy I am? Tomorrow, we'll look for a new apartment...no, we'll drive out into the country and buy a big house and...

LINDA

But, how...how is this possible?

MICHAEL

Oh, I see...you think I'm crazy? Of course! *It's all crazy!* Well, in a nutshell...I met a man tonight, an old friend, and...and he helped me...*he helped us!* I don't know how, but he knew all about my troubles and yours. God knows. But, he came like Fate and gave me his checkbook and said the sky's the limit and...then, he led me here and pointed to your door. The door of the child he loved...

LINDA

What?

MICHAEL

Do you remember when you used to talk to the man who had his lunch every day in Central Park? By the zoo? Do you remember?

LINDA

Oh yes!

MICHAEL

He said you would. *How?* I don't know. If I didn't know any better, I'd think he was some kind of archangel. No, this man among men, this friend...his name is James. James Younger.

LINDA

But, that is *my* name! Linda Younger.

MICHAEL

How can that be? Is it a coincidence?

LINDA

I was a child, I remember. My grandmother used to take me to the park...to meet with him ...and I talked with him on the bench near the zoo. But, I never knew who he was...

MICHAEL

Your *father!* He said your parents were divorced. He was talking about *himself* all the time. Your mother must have kept you away from him. Those times at the park...your grandmother must have sneaked you there to see him...

LINDA

But, I never knew why! Then, we moved away. I never saw him again. And, then, my grandmother died. And, my mother died...*Bring him to me!*

MICHAEL

I don't know..

LINDA

How can he know I am here and stay away! Does he think I have forgotten? Is he embarrassed to see me?

MICHAEL

No, no...

LINDA

Bring him to me! Oh, the happiness you have brought! I love you! I promise you we will live in happiness forever. Now bring him to me!

MICHAEL

I'll try...

(MUSIC, STREET NOISE, BAR NOISE)

What am I going to do? I don't see him around. He might have left town for all I know. Bartender? *Bartender !* Let me ask you a question...you know Mr. Younger? James Younger?

BARTENDER

Yeah, Mr. Younger. I know him for a long time. But, he hasn't been around here for at least a month. Maybe, six weeks.

MICHAEL

What are you talking about? I was just in here with him around eight o'clock.

BARTENDER

No, you were here alone.

MICHAEL

Alone? But, you served us. Martinis.

BARTENDER

You ordered two martinis, but, you were alone. I figured you had one too many. You were talking to yourself. Then, you broke a glass. But, you paid for it.

MICHAEL

I was *alone?* That can't be. He was standing right next to me when I broke the glass. Maybe, the other bartender saw him. Can you ask him to come over.

BARTENDER
Hey Charley!   When was the last time Mr. Younger was in
here?

CHARLEY
Mr. Younger? Why you want to know?

MICHAEL
I was in here with him earlier tonight.

CHARLEY
You were here earlier tonight with Mr. Younger?

MICHAEL
Yeah. But, if he comes in again, tomorrow, whenever....maybe
I can leave my phone number here and...

CHARLEY
Mr. Younger won't be calling you, mister.

MICHAEL
What are you talking about? Why not?

CHARLEY
Sorry to have to break it to you...but, Mr. Younger was killed
over a month ago...

MICHAEL
Killed?

CHARLEY
Hit and run. Some place out in Queens. Never caught the
bastard.

MICHAEL
Hit and run?

CHARLEY
Sorry about that. Say, you look like you need a drink. Here, sit
down, have a martini...it's on the house.

A DAY DREAM
By Dan Bianchi
From A Story By Fitz-James O'Brien

Cast – 2m
Length – 15 min
Synopsis – A man contemplates killing his friend

DANNY

Feel like a stroll down to the Five Points tonight?

NARRATOR

I don't think so. I, for one, value my life. Too much murder going on down at Five Points nowadays. The other morning, a respectable man who keeps a quiet, orderly bordello... under the supervision of a middle-aged female of irreproachable morals....he's found hacked to pieces in his room. And, on every street corner, gangs of ruffians are ready to strangle or knife any passerby who has three cents on him. The police are everywhere, but, where they ought to be. No, I don't think I'll be going down there any time soon.

DANNY

But, there's no danger. We will go with Captain Currycomb of the 150th ward. As efficient an officer, let me tell you, Sir, as any in the city of New York. He will show us everything, and I'd like to see the man that would touch us while under his protection. Besides, look here.

NARRATOR

What's that? A revolver?

DANNY

Exquisite, ain't it? Look at that handle...ivory and silver, that is. And, small enough to hide in any pocket. Go on, hold it. Feel that silky lock. Pass your fingers over the polished stock. Feels good , don't it? Look at that barrel, delicate, ain't it? See the way the light plays off the surface, like a blue mirror...

NARRATOR

"Suddenly...I find myself in a daydream, speculating on what

would occur if I were to shoot my friend. I see the precise spot in his temple...a little above the left eyebrow...where the bullet would enter. I see the sudden spasm...almost invisible, so slight is it...that convulses his frame as the ball strikes him. The rapid flash of the eye on me...so rapid that we have no term to measure it with...one glance of terror, reproach, *amazement*...Now, his legs bend, and, double up under him as if the bones have been suddenly withdrawn... he rolls on the floor. Strange. He lays on the floor with his body bent forward, his forehead touching the earth, and his arms extended in front. Like a Moslem at prayer with his head toward the Holy City. I remember a picture of that in one of my childhood books. A Turk at his devotions. But, my friend is not praying. He's dead. Almost instantly. That last fleeting look he gave me was the flash of his passing soul. Lying there on the carpet...a white carpet with a pattern of ivy leaves trailing across it. And, now, a small scarlet stream that slowly, *slowly* flows from his temple, until it reaches a bunch of ivy leaves, where it spreads into a little round pool. Like a cluster of red berries clinging to the plant. Now, hold on a second. I've just committed a murder. It's no longer just a curious incident to me...in *fact*, it's beginning to make me *quite* agitated. My heart is beating like a drum. Cold sweat on my brow. My friend, my *dead* friend, perhaps, he's not praying at all...perhaps, he lies there in that odd position ready to spring up at me. Like some dark fiend. Wanting to *destroy* me. I have to get out of here, quickly. But, the corpse...it's somehow blocking my way to get out. And, I keep stepping in the pool of blood and tracking it across the rug. I can't take my boots off! They're glued to my feet. Try scraping the blood off on the grate in the fireplace!
Yes! *No!* It's not working. The blood is *too* wet. I'm still leaving footprints all over the floor. What am I to do?
                                                                  (KNOCKING)

"Someone at the door? *Now?* Should I answer it? No.
                                                        (KNOCKING
                                        LOUDER, DOOR, LOCK RATTLING)

"It's going to burst open any second! *The window!* Oh my God, it's fifty feet to the alley below. *The door!* Throw yourself against it.
                                        (WOOD STRAINING, CRACKING)

"Can't last much longer! Every muscle, straining...what can it be? I can't...*I can't...*"

DANNY
So, can I have my pistol back, now?

NARRATOR
What? Oh, certainly. Here. I don't really like to have guns around, anyway.

DANNY
Afraid of what you might do with one if you had the chance?

NARRATOR
Me? No. Well, are we going down to Five Points with Captain Currycomb, or not?

DANNY
Sure. For a minute there, I gotta tell you, when you were cocking the pistol, you had a wild look in your eyes.

NARRATOR
Who, *me?* Oh, don't be ridiculous.

DANNY
The feel of a gun can sometimes do that to some people.

NARRATOR
"I laughed and said nothing."

THE BEAST IN THE CAVE
By Dan Bianchi
From A Story By H.P. Lovecraft

Cast – 2m
Length – 15 min
Synopsis – A lost cave explorer discovers a creature in the dark

(CAVE DRIPPING, ECHOING
THROUGHOUT STORY)

NARRATOR

(ECHO) Hello! Can anyone hear me? "I'm lost. Completely, hopelessly lost in Mammoth Cave. In this vast labyrinth. Wandering for an hour. Every direction I turn…I can't find any familiar objects or paths to the way out. I'm beginning to believe I shall never see daylight again. Losing hope. Luckily, I'm not the frantic sort. I'd be pulling out my hair, screaming bloody murder by now. My fault. I had to wander away from our tour. I've gone too far now. No search party is going to find me. If I must die, then, I guess this terrible cavern will be my tomb. I'll probably starve to death down here. My flashlight is nearly dead. Soon I'll be enveloped by total blackness here in the bowels of the Earth. I never imagined I'd die in Kentucky. Just an hour and fifteen minutes ago…I was staring in awe at a row of cottages the guide was showing us….built in the caverns years ago by a colony of consumptives, who thought the atmosphere in the underground world would be beneficial to their health. Can you imagine? Living down here. Like mole people. That's what the guide called them. Now, I shall join them in death down here. My light is flickering…the batteries are dying. I must try everything left in my power to escape." (ECHO) Help! Is anyone there? Can you hear me? *Help!* "Nothing. They might be miles away. *Damn!* There goes the light. Darkness. Pitch black darkness. Well…it's all over now. Wait…what's that?

(SOFT FOOTSTEPS ON ROCKS)

"Can someone have heard me? Come to my rescue so soon? Maybe, I'm not as far away from people as I think? They might have been just over the ridge all this time!" *Hello?* Is someone there?

(ODD MUTTERING SOUNDS, ROCKS SHIFT)

Hel...lo? "It suddenly occurs to me...I *know* the sound of boots on rocks, sharp, incisive blows. These sounds...they *aren't* boots...more like... *padded paws*...and there aren't two feet....but, *four! A mountain lion!* Oh my God...a mountain lion stalking me in the darkness....looks like I'm not going to die from starvation after all! Have to remain quiet. Quiet. Still. Maybe it can't see me. It'll pass me by in the dark. No...no... it's coming for me....right *at* me. I need a weapon! A rock ...reach down and grab a loose boulder...that's it. If it comes any closer...wait for the right moment now...getting closer ...Stopped. What's it doing? Is it standing right in front of me? Should I strike out at it? Maybe, it can see in the dark...like a bat? *It* can see *me*, I can't see *it. Great!* I have to remain dead still. Listen! Listen with all my might! Even if I kill it, I don't even know what it looks like. Now, I wish I smoked cigarettes. I'd have matches. The tension is murdering me. Every muscle is trembling. I think it's really close now. A few feet. Getting closer. Should I scream? I want to. I don't think I can. My nerves are petrified. I can't move. I don't even know if I can lift my arm to strike it with this rock. Listen...it's on the move. Oh my God, oh my God, I can hear it breathing. It sounds...tired, out of breath. That's it, time to strike!" *Die you bastard!*

(ROCKS SHIFT, CRUNCH)

"Did I hit it? Did I hit it? Where did it go?

(ROCKS SHIFT)

"No...it's still there. Still there." I hear you. *DIE! DIE! DIE!*

(ECHO. NOISE)

"I think that did it. Yes...I'm sure I hit it that time. It's down, I think. I've injured it. Maybe I killed it? Listen...listen..."

(BREATHING)

"No, it's still alive. But, it does sound wounded. Should I try to find it? Maybe I should bash its skull in...kill it altogether? No, stay away from that thing. Whatever it is. In fact...get out of here. Get going! *Run!* Anywhere!"

(FOOTSTEPS RUN, ROCKS SHIFT)

"Oh God, God, help me. I can't go on. Bruised, battered, smashing against rocks...I must be bleeding in a hundred places. I'm going to wind up running off a cliff down here. Might as well. Where the hell am I? Hell?

(CLICKING SOUND)

"Hey... I know that sound. That's a pick axe...the *tour guide!"* (ECHOES) *Hello! Help! I'm over here!* "A light! *A light*!" I see you! I'm over here! *Here!* Can you hear me? "Run, run toward the light. It's the guide, I can see him!" *I see you!*

GUIDE
(Distant) Hello there!

NARRATOR
Thank God, I'm rescued! Oh thank you, thank you, thank you! I want to thank you from the bottom of my heart. Really. I must, sorry if I'm a complete jabbering idiot. But, you see, I'm sure I killed something back there. With a rock. I know I did. It attacked me, I'm sure and then, I ran a bit, but...when I saw you coming my way...sorry for all the gibbering...

GUIDE
No need. Here, have some water. I'm only glad I noticed you'd gone missing from the group...you'd have been a goner for sure.

NARRATOR
You don't have to tell me. I had it figured I'd die down here. Sorry about that.

GUIDE
These passages are highly dangerous even for professionals. Why, we've had a whole bunch of disappearances down here in the past few years. Everybody thinks they're seasoned explorers. *Spelunkers*, they call themselves. They got no business coming down here alone. Fall off a cliff, down a ravine, stuck in some tiny crevasse...gone. We don't even *find* the bodies. We used to find the bodies. Not anymore.

NARRATOR

Why?

GUIDE

It's a mystery to me. Explorers keep going deeper into the caves. Even the old timers like me don't know those parts. They just disappear. So, you say you ran this way over here, right?

NARRATOR

Yeah, just a bit. I must have come down this path.

GUIDE

And, you think you killed some animal?

NARRATOR

Maybe, wounded it.

GUIDE

What kind of animal?

NARRATOR

I don't know. I'm not sure. A mountain lion, maybe? I heard it breathing. Listen, I know you must think I'm crazy. It's just back there.

GUIDE

People can get spooked in total darkness. I just don't see how a mountain lion could survive down here. There are fish in some of the streams, blind fish, but, lions don't eat fish. But, I guess if it had to, it might adapt. Stranger things have happened. Adaptation. Survival of the fittest and all that. Look, we'll search a few minutes more, but, then we'd better turn back.

NARRATOR

Sure, sure. Just scan your light over that way...from left to right...I'm sure it was around here...

GUIDE

Damn! Will you look at that!

NARRATOR

There it is!

GUIDE

What is that thing?   It's whiter than the limestone.

NARRATOR

Let's see!

(ROCKS SHIFT)

GUIDE

Hey, hey...careful now.

NARRATOR

What the hell is it?

GUIDE

It's no mountain lion.

NARRATOR

It resembles an ape...maybe it escaped from some traveling carnival and found its way in here?

GUIDE

Yeah, right. That's even weirder than it being a mountain lion. It's albino, whatever it is...its hair is snow white...

NARRATOR

Maybe, it's one of those sasquatch?

GUIDE

Look how long that white hair is...on its head...down around its shoulders.

NARRATOR

It's very thin. Can't see the face...it's turned downward.

GUIDE

Look how long its arms are. And its legs...did it walk upright?

NARRATOR

I don't know. It was total darkness. Maybe it did. Sounded like it was on all fours.

GUIDE

It's got long claws on its fingers. I don't see any kind of tail. Don't get too close now.

NARRATOR

Hey! It's still breathing…barely.

GUIDE

Maybe I should shoot it…put it out of its misery.

(GROAN)

NARRATOR

That doesn't sound like any ape.

GUIDE

Or anything I've ever heard.

NARRATOR

Maybe, it hasn't made a sound in such a long time…it's trying to for the first time? Maybe it's crying out…like I was…for help?

GUIDE

Look at that…the whole body is shaking, trembling. Limbs contracting. Death spasm, that's what that is. Watch out…it's rolling over! Oh no…*no*…my God, no.

NARRATOR

What? Let me see! Look at those black eyes…they're staring at me…That nose…that's not an ape nose. Its mouth… opening…

(GROANING)

It's trying to speak!

GUIDE

Nah…It's dead.

NARRATOR

Dead.

GUIDE

Stop staring at it.   We have to get out of here.

NARRATOR

That thing…it was trying to speak…that creature I killed is no strange beast…*it's a man!*

GUIDE

Well, it might have been…at one time or another. Or, maybe its parents were human.

NARRATOR

You mean…that colony that lived down here? All those years ago?

(DISTANT NOISES, GRUNTS, ROCKS)

GUIDE

Adaptation, remember? Listen to that…I think we'd better get going…real fast.

NARRATOR

But, we need to carry him out of here…or, at least, bury him…

(DISTANT GRUNTS, SCREAMS GROW LOUDER)

GUIDE

No time for that. Listen! You hear that? He isn't alone. There must be more of them. And they're getting closer…

NARRATOR

More of them?

GUIDE

Oh God…Now I know what happened to those bodies…the explorers that had gone missing…!

NARRATOR

More of them? They must be coming for him.

GUIDE
You fool! They're not coming for him! *They're coming for us!*
And they're probably hungry as hell!   Run! *Run!*
(MUSIC. GRUNTING.
GUN SHOTS. SCREAMS)

NIGHTMARE HOUSE
By Dan Bianchi
From A Story By Edward Lucas White

Cast – 3m
Length – 20 min
Synopsis – A hiker spends the night in an abandoned house

(MUSIC, COUNTRY SOUNDS, BIRDS)

NARRATOR

"There it is. The one with the slate roof. Right under the brow of the mountain smack in the middle of the woods. Can barely see the roof as the sun is sinking behind the far blue hills. I've been seeing bits of that house all day as I hike in that direction through the farms, up the steep mountains, along the old dirt roads. Always changing angles, but, I manage to catch sight of it all day long. Tall trees surrounding it, an orchard across the road. Those trees form straight, even rows. There's a cinder side path and a low stone wall. What's that? On the orchard side between two of the flanking trees is a white object. Looks like a tall stone, I suppose. Lots of lime stones in this region. I think I'll see for myself.

(MUSIC)

"Damn, my legs are about to give out.   I've been hiking through these forests on this treacherous mountainside for days now. Haven't seen a decent place to stay in quite awhile. Only wretched cabins by the road. The slate roof house is just up this road. And, there's the tall stone. Well, that *is* something, isn't it? I could have sworn it was *opposite* the house next to the orchard...but, clearly, it's on the left-hand side of the road *next* to the house. Oh, well. In another fifteen minutes or so, I should be there.

(MUSIC)

"Coming round the bend in the road now and...well, don't that beat all? The tall stone...am I going screwy? Now, it's on the *right* of the road. *Next* to the orchard. Don't ask me. Maybe my eyes are going. There's the mountain I just came down off of behind me...and there goes the last ray of the sun just about to disappear. Some clouds coming in...maybe, rain on the way...and there's the house, the slate roof and the road and...oh no! That can't be. The tall stone...*no*. It's...on the...*left* side now. I mean, I only looked away for a second. This can't be. Someone is playing tricks on me. Next it will be in the *middle* of the road! You see, this is what happens when you go hiking alone! Get a grip on yourself! *Look!* There's a boy up ahead. Standing at the edge of the cinder path. A stocky kid, barefoot, trousers rolled up to his knees. No coat, no hat. Blonde, freckled. And, Lord a mighty, he's got a hideous harelip. He's shifting from foot to foot, staring at me, but, he's not saying anything. Guess they don't have many visitors out here." Hello! How far is it to a town?

BOY

Eight mile.

NARRATOR

"That cleft palate of his...I can hardly understand him." Can you drive me there?

BOY

No team on the place...no horse, no cow.

NARRATOR

How far to the next house?

BOY

Six mile.

NARRATOR

Six miles? It's already dark. Nearly seven thirty. May I sleep in your house tonight?

BOY

You can come in if you want to and sleep if you can. House all messy... ma's been dead three year, and dad's away. Nothin' to eat but buckwheat flour and rusty bacon.

NARRATOR

I've got enough to eat. In my sack.

BOY

You can come in if you've a mind to.

NARRATOR

All right, lead the way. "The yard in front of the house is dark under a dozen or more immense willow trees. Below these are many smaller trees. Deep, shaggy, matted grass. This driveway looks to have once been a carriage path, a curved driveway, leading to the house. Now, buried under weeds and tall grass. The house is grey stone with green shutters... faded almost as grey as the stone. There's a porch, no railing. A few old rocking chairs. A wide door. We stand here awhile." Can you open the door?

BOY

Open it yourself.

NARRATOR

Oh, well, alright.

(DOOR CREAKS OPEN)

"We walk into the hall. *Phew!* It stinks of mold and dampness. There are several doors on either side."

BOY

You can have that room. Go on, open it.

(DOOR CREAKS OPEN)

NARRATOR

Better get a lamp.

BOY

No lamp. No candle. Mostly I get abed before dark.

NARRATOR

Alright then. I've got a few candles. "The boy just stands there in the doorway. Watching me. I light a candle. The walls are white-washed, the floor bare. Can't escape that mildew, phew! Oddly enough, the bed looks freshly made up and clean. A bit clammy. There's nothing else in the room but two old chairs and a small table. I raise a window to let in some air." Can you show me to the kitchen? "So, with my candle in hand, I follow him through the hail to the back of the house. The kitchen is large, a few pine chairs, a bench and table. No stove, only a big hearth. The ashes look about a month old. I go out the back to the woodshed to grab a log or two. I notice that the axe and hatchet are both rusty and dull, but usable, so I quickly make myself a roaring fire. To my amazement, on a hot July evening like this, the boy with a wry smile on his ugly face, leans over the flame, hands and arms spread out, and fairly roasts himself." Are you cold?

                         BOY
I'm always cold.

                       NARRATOR
Careful. Don't scorch yourself. Any water around here?

                         BOY
Pump out back.

                       NARRATOR
"I discover the pump, which, luckily, is in working order.
                                    (PUMPS WATER)

"But, I have a helluva time filling two leaky pails. Back at the hearth in the kitchen I put water to boil and set the table with my own meal...cold chicken, cold ham, white and brown bread, olives, jam, and cake. I even made hot soup. And coffee too." Won't you join me? I've got plenty.

                         BOY
I ain't hungry. I've had supper.

                       NARRATOR
"The kid looks like he's starving and he's turning down food like this? Standing there, staring. Now, I'm not feeling so hungry anymore." I think I'll sit out on the porch in one of those hickory rockers and have a smoke. "The boy follows me silently and seats himself on the porch floor, leaning against a pillar, his feet on the grass outside." What do you do when your father is away?

BOY

Just loaf 'round.   Just fool 'round.

NARRATOR

How far off are your nearest neighbors?

BOY

Don't no neighbors never come here. Say they're afeared of the ghosts.

NARRATOR

Well, I must admit...this house of yours can lead one to believe it's haunted. Do you ever see any ghosts around here?

BOY

I never see 'em. Never hear 'em. Sort o' feel 'em 'round sometimes.

NARRATOR

Are you afraid of them?

BOY

Nope, I ain't skeered o' ghosts...I'm skeered o' nightmares. Ever have nightmares?

NARRATOR

Very seldom.

BOY

I do. Always have the same nightmare...big sow, big as a steer, trying to eat me up. Wake up so skeered I could run forever. Nowheres to run to. Go to sleep, and have it again. Wake up worse skeered than ever. Dad says it's buckwheat cakes in summer.

NARRATOR

You must have teased a sow some time and now it's haunting you.

BOY

Yep. Teased a big sow once, holding up one of her pigs by the hind leg. Teased her too long. Fell in the pen and got bit up some. Wisht I hadn't a' teased her. Have that nightmare three times a week sometimes. Worse'n being burnt out. Worse'n ghosts. Say, I sorter feel ghosts around now.

NARRATOR

Oh yeah? You're not trying to frighten me?   "A moment later, I feel this odd sensation, like some light fabric trailing across my face." Did you do that?

BOY

Ain't done nothing. What was it?

NARRATOR

It was like a piece of mosquito-netting brushed over my face.

BOY

That ain't netting. That's a veil. That's one of the ghosts. Some blow on you... some touch you with their long, cold fingers. That one with the veil she drags acrossed your face...well, mostly I think it's ma.

NARRATOR

Oh, you think so? Well...I'm getting tired now. Think I'll turn in. Good night.

BOY

Good night.   I'll sit out here a spell yet.

NARRATOR

"Ghosts, huh? The boy is just trying to scare me, that's all. His mother's veil? Hmmm. Maybe I should just leave the candle burning awhile until I fall asleep. The bed has a comfortable mattress. Yes...sleep...get some sleep...

(MUSIC)

"Oh, I sleep alright. But, it's not a quiet sleep by no means. A terrible nightmare...the same as the boy had described.

(PIG GRUNTS, SCREAMS)

"A huge sow, big as a work horse, rearing up with her forelegs over the foot-board of the bed, trying to scramble over to me. She grunts and puffs, and I feel she's craving to eat me! Even in the dream, I know it's a dream, so I try my damnest to wake myself up. Just as the gigantic dream-beast flounders over the foot-board, falling across my shins, I awake... *Ahhh!* Only to find I am in absolute darkness, as if sealed in a bank vault. Have to calm myself. Calm down. Don't panic. You know where you are. So, I return to sleep again. But, this time...the nightmare is worse than ever before. *Pure horror!* So real, so real it is. There is a *Thing* in the room...not a sow, some creature, I don't know what it is... a *Thing.* Big as an elephant, filling the room to the ceiling. Shaped like a wild boar, seated on its haunches, with its forelegs braced stiffly in front of it. A hot, slobbering, red mouth, full of big tusks, and its jaws working hungrily. It shuffles and hunches itself forward, inch by inch, till its vast forelegs straddle the bed.

(PIG GRUNTS ECHO, WOOD SPLITTING)

"The bed is crushed up like wet blotting-paper... and I feel the weight of the Thing on my feet, on my legs, on my *body*, on my chest. It's hungry, and *I* am what it is hungry for, and it means to begin on my face. Its dripping mouth grows nearer and nearer. I can't move, can't call out. I'm helpless! *Helpless!*

(MUSIC, ROOSTER CROWS)

"I'm alive. I'm here. I know where I am. The wooden chairs, the cracked dirty window panes. Thank God it's morning. Quickly, I get dressed and I'm out into the hall." Hello! "I realize I don't even know the boy's name." *Hello!* "No answer. Well, I've had enough of this house. I can still feel the after effects of that terrible nightmare. I'm not about to go searching for the kid. I take a swallow of cold coffee and munch a biscuit I've left on the table from the night before. Here, here's a silver dollar for his trouble. I'll leave it here on the table so he can't miss it. The sun's coming up now. I make my way out to the road. The tall, white stone...there it is again. Standing like a sentinel. Either on the left of the road, or, the right, I don't give a damn. Well, the boy said the town is off this way about six miles. Let's get to it.

(MUSIC)

"It's been about an hour out here in the hot sun. I feel as if I've already walked ten miles. There's a house, the first house I've seen that looks inhabited. Neatly painted and close to the road, with a whitewashed fence along its front garden."

(DOG WOOFS)

Oh oh. Nice boy! Nice dog! "Alright, he's wagging his tail and regarding me with a friendly eye. But, I don't think I'll enter the gate." Hey mister. Will your dog bite?

MAN
Naw, he barks but he don't bite. Come in.

NARRATOR
I've been out hiking in the hills here. I got down here in the valley about sunset last night so I stayed in the house down the road.

MAN
You did what? That there house is *haunted!* They say if you have to go past it after dark, you can't tell which side of the road the big white stone is on.

NARRATOR
I couldn't tell even before sunset.

MAN
There! And you *slept* in that house! Did you sleep, honest?

NARRATOR
Well...I did have this nightmare.

MAN
See? I wouldn't go in there if it meant my holy salvation. And you slept! How in thunder did you get in?

NARRATOR
The boy took me in.

MAN
What sort of boy?

NARRATOR
A heavy-set, freckle-faced boy with a harelip.

MAN

Talks like his mouth is full of mush?

NARRATOR

Yes, bad case of cleft palate.

MAN

Well! Don't that beat all? I never did believe in ghosts, and I never did half believe that house was haunted, but, I know it now. And, you slept!

NARRATOR

Well, I didn't see any ghosts.

MAN

Mister...you seen a ghost for sure. That there harelip boy's been dead six months. Fell in a hog pen and they chewed him up bad. His father got crazy over it and killed all the hogs and then he killed himself.

NARRATOR

Really? Well, yeah, I guess...I can believe it's haunted alright. But, what's that big white rock moving around out there on the road? What's all that about?

MAN

Mister...I have no idea. Just count yourself lucky you're here to even ask.

THE TERROR BY NIGHT
By Dan Bianchi

Cast – 2m, 2w
Length – 15 min
Synopsis – A traveler is attacked in a small town

(HORSE APPROACHES, STOPS, WHINNIES)

NARRATOR

Hello!

GIRL

Hello! What are you doing way out here?

NARRATOR

I've been out hiking all day. I'm afraid I've lost my way. Do you know how far it is back to Holbrook?

GIRL

It's getting dark. You won't make it before sunset.

NARRATOR

Oh. I was afraid of that. Well, I was just about to sit and have a sandwich. Want to join me?

GIRL

Well, I am tired, and hungry, too. Have you enough for us both?

NARRATOR

Sure! Come and rest a moment. I've got a fire going here. Heating up some water for hot tea. Even have a shot of whiskey if you prefer. I've got ham and cheese sandwiches.

GIRL

Great. I've been out riding all afternoon. I'm hopelessly late for dinner, and I've still got miles to go. Poor old Tybalt, he could use the rest. But, I can't stay long. But you...how are you going to get back to Holbrook? It's dangerous out here at night.

NARRATOR

I didn't bring camping gear. I thought I'd be back just about now. Well, it's not the first time I've slept on hard ground. What? You look serious. You don't approve?

GIRL

People don't, as a rule, sleep out...about here.

NARRATOR

No?

GIRL

Are you superstitious?

NARRATOR

As a rule, no. Why?

GIRL

Don't laugh. There is a legend...people about here say that the hills here are haunted. There is a Thing that hunts people to death!

NARRATOR

(Laughs) Really! Has anyone been caught by this *thing?*

GIRL

Yes, old George Tobias. He was one of Dad's patients...he's the village doctor...George worked on a farm, a big purple-faced man, who drank a lot. They found him in a ditch with his clothes all torn and covered with mud. He had been run to death... there was no wound on his body...died of heart failure. See that big stone up there on top of the hill?

NARRATOR

Yes...hmmm, that's odd, just sitting there alone like that.

GIRL

People say that's an altar of sorts.

NARRATOR

An altar?

GIRL

From way back. Before the white man came here. Blood sacrifices were made there on that altar.

NARRATOR

Really? So, you think some heathen god is going to come and get me here in the dark?

GIRL

Don't laugh. The people about here are superstitious...but they have their reasons.

NARRATOR

No, I don't mean to laugh. But, this is 1920. You're talking about hundreds of years ago. It's a little hard to believe in something evil about this place...it's so beautiful. Tell me, is there any charm or incantation, just in case...?

GIRL

They say iron...cold iron...is the only thing it cannot cross. Well, I have to be off...Thank you for your generosity. Really, though, I don't think I should stay here if I were you. *Please!*

NARRATOR

Oh, I'll be alright! Good bye! Maybe we shall meet again!
                                    (HORSE RIDES OFF. OWL, NIGHT SOUNDS,
                                                    FIRE CRACKLES)

"Hmm, it is kind of spooky out here. That big rock up there, outlined against the sunset. Maybe, I should start walking...the moon's come up. But, out here...

                                                    (BIRD SCREECH)

"What's that? Nerves on edge, old boy. Pretty soon, you'll be joining the superstitious folk around here, believing in bogey men roaming the woods. Look at you, trembling like a school girl. Heart beating a mile a minute. Wait...ugh, what's that smell? *Ycch*...like some dead animal...
                                    (STONES SHIFT, BRANCHES CRUNCH)

"What? Who? Someone is definitely there." *Hello!* "Can't see a thing."

(CRUNCH)

Hello? "I think…I'd better run. *Run!* I'm running!

(RUNNING)

"Where am I going? I can't see a thing! Just run, just go! Far away! Something right behind me! I can hear it! I can hear it breathing! Right on my heels! I can't stop to look around. I don't even want to know what it is! You can outrun him, whatever it is. You were a champion in college. Well, now you're running for your life!

(CRASH INTO BRUSH)

"Oh! My ankle! Must …have hit a rabbit hole! Damn! Keep going…where is it? *Where is it?* It's over to the right of me…moving through the bushes…*no!* Now it's at my elbow I can smell it, God! It stinks! This *Thing*…it's playing with me! Hunting me…sporting with me. God help me! It can get me anytime it wants.

(MUSIC)

"Where am I? Feel like my leg is on fire…the pain. My watch…I smashed it. I don't even know…what…where is that thing? It's out there. Oh, my leg. Killing me. I can't keep this up.

(MUSIC)

"If I was lost before, I'm…but, still on a road. Where is that thing? I can hear it…can't see it. *Lights!* Lights, far ahead. A village! Thank God! But, the fog's setting in. I'm losing the road.

(MUSIC)

"I can't…I can't…never make it to the village…just give up…take me…I can't out run it…any…longer…*Come on!* Come and get me! Look…look…is that a house…looks like a garage…no, a blacksmith…yes…yes…

GIRL (V.O.)
There's a Thing that hunts people to death. But iron…cold iron …it cannot cross.

NARRATOR

Getting closer...closer...I'm gonna make it...

(DOG BARKING)

Gonna...ohh!

(MUSIC)

GIRL

Dad, I just heard in the village. I came right away. How's your patient?

DOCTOR

Strange. He's in shock. Severe exhaustion and shock, heart strained, superficial lesions, bruises, scratches, and so forth. Mentally, he is in a great state of excitement and terror... lapsing into delirium at times. I've given him a sedative. But, that's only temporary. I'm afraid he'll need to be taken to a sanitarium. It's most mysterious...

GIRL

Do you think I might see him for a minute?

DOCTOR

Why? Do you know this man?

GIRL

I met him yesterday while I was riding. I may be able to help you diagnose his illness.

DOCTOR

Well, he requires rest, careful nursing, absolute quiet...

GIRL

He can stay with us. In the guest house. Until he can go to hospital.

DOCTOR

Well, I suppose...ah, here's Mrs.Thompson...

GIRL

Hello, Dorothy...

MRS.THOMPSON
These men. They never listen. Think they can do what they want when it comes to...*eh!* Think they're so big and strong. But, it won't do against the...I warn them all the time. Don't go roaming the hills after dark. No, nothing can hurt them. It was the iron that saved him.

GIRL
What?

MRS.THOMPSON
He came running into the yard and tripped over a pile of iron bars my husband throws in a pile out there and there he was lying on the ground, bleeding. We wouldn't have known if the dog hadn't woke us. If it wasn't for the iron, the cold iron...he wouldn't be lying in there still breathing, that's for sure.
(TEA KETTLE WHISTLE)

Oh, there's the kettle. I'm forgetting I put on the tea.
(DOOR OPENS)

GIRL
Hello...

NARRATOR
Hello...

GIRL
You don't look so well.

NARRATOR
Go on... say it!

GIRL
Say what?

NARRATOR
Say, *I told you so!*

GIRL
I told you that cold iron...

NARRATOR

Cold iron saved me. Well, *you* saved me… last night.

GIRL

Yes, I did. But, in the future…

NARRATOR

Oh, have no fear of that. I won't be needing cold iron again.
Except for a ton of automobile driving as fast as it can back to
New York City.

GIRL

Where, I suppose, you'll be making fun of our rural
superstitions to all of your sophisticated friends.

NARRATOR

Between you and me…I promise never to mention again what
happened last night…for the rest of my life.

GIRL

So…does that make you a believer, now? (Pause) I said…does
that make you a believer now? *Oh no…Dad!* Dad come in
here!

DOCTOR

What?

MRS.THOMPSON

Is he dead yet?

GIRL

He…he's not breathing…

DOCTOR

Yes…I'm afraid…he's gone.

GIRL

What did you give him?

DOCTOR

Don't worry. It was painless. And quick.

MRS.THOMPSON

He's dead?

DOCTOR

Yes.

GIRL

I wish we didn't have to...

DOCTOR

There's nothing we could do...if he had left here telling stories
...we'd have everyone in the world descending on us, strangers
looking to ridicule us...

MRS.THOMPSON

Busy bodies. City folk. Non Believers. Did he die...a believer?

GIRL

He didn't say. But, after all he went through...I should think he
did.

MRS.THOMPSON

No matter. We'll give him a proper send off. I'll prepare the
body. My husband and the men have already gone to get the
altar ready...we haven't had a sacrifice in a long time...

DOCTOR

It's been awhile since the last...

GIRL

No wonder the thing was out for blood last night...

THE DOOR IN THE WALL
By Dan Bianchi
From A Story By H.G.Wells

Cast – 2m
Length – 30 min
Synopsis – A man is forever haunted by a door only he sees

NARRATOR

"Wallace Greenaway the Third. Not the sort of person you might care to remember. But, one can't choose one's memories. I can still see him. That look he had, that look of detachment. Yes, when the interest left him, he forgot all about you. But, the interest was not *always* out of him, and, when he had his mind set on something, he'd be extremely successful at it. In High School, he *collected* scholarships. His career, indeed, appeared to be successful. Passed me by long ago. Became a national figure before he was forty. People still say that he could have been President, someday… *if* he had lived.

(MUSIC)

"It was at college where Wallace first told me about the *Door In The Wall*. I didn't pay much mind to it. The other time I heard of it was only a month before Wallace died. To him, at least, the Door in the Wall was a *real* door leading through a *real* wall to immortal realities. And, it came into his life early, when he was a little fellow between five and six. I remember, in those final days, how Wallace told, or, confessed, the story to me…"

WALLACE

There was a red vine, a Virginia creeper all around it…the white wall. Horse chestnut leaves, yellow and green, on the pavement. Must be October. And, the door, the green door. I'm…five years and four months old.

NARRATOR

"I assumed that he was a rather precocious little boy…learned to talk at an abnormally early age, and he was so sane and *old-fashioned*, as people say, that he was permitted an amount of initiative that most children scarcely attain by seven or eight. His mother died when he was born, and he was under the care of a governess. His father was a stern, preoccupied lawyer, who gave him little attention, and expected great things of him. For all his brightness, little Wallace found life a bit grey and dull, I think. And, so, one day he wandered."

WALLACE

I don't know how I got away. Nor, what roads I took...can't remember. It's all a blur. But, I do remember the white wall and the green door. Oh yes. Quite clearly. That's certain. The first time I saw it...it made me feel something...an emotion, an attraction, a *desire* to get to that door and open it and walk in. As if it was calling me. But, at the same time, a voice inside me warned me against it. But, the door...well, it seemed to be unlocked. Still, what about my father? He would be very angry with me if I proceeded to enter. I hesitated and walked on past that door...straight to a town, a poor little place, dirty windows, dusty stores. I pretended to occupy myself by browsing among tawdry bric-a-brac and old plumbing supplies and cans of paint. All the while, I'm standing there, thinking of the green door. That's it! I can't stand it any longer.

(FOOTSTEPS RUNNING)

I sprint right back to that green door, open it and...and, in that moment, I came into the garden that has haunted me all my life. I can't describe it, not really. There is something in the very air of it that's exhilarating... gives one a sense of lightness and good happening and well-being... something in the *sight* of it that makes all its color clean and perfect...glowing. That's it, *glowing*. I feel glad. Joyful. Everything is beautiful here. And, look *there!*

(PURRING)

There are two great leopards. Yes, it's true, spotted leopards. But, I'm not afraid. They're just playing there on the wide path with marble-edged flower borders on either side. Two huge velvety beasts playing with a ball. One looks up, he's coming toward me now....curious, I suppose. Right up to me. Rubbing his soft round ear very gently against the small hand I hold out and he's purring. I tell you, this is an enchanted garden. It stretches as far as the horizon. It feels as if I've come home.

(DOOR SLAMS)

Suddenly, the door closes behind me

(DOOR SLAMS SHUT)

and I forget the road and its fallen chestnut leaves, the town,
the shops, my house with the governess and father... I forget
all hesitations and fear, forget discretion, forget all the intimate
realities of this life. I've become a very *happy* little boy...in
another world. A world with a different quality, a warmer, more
penetrating and mellower light, with a gladness in its air, and
wisps of sun-touched clouds in the blueness of its sky. And,
before me, this long wide path, flower beds on either side, rich
with untended flowers, and these two great leopards. I put my
little hands, fearlessly, on their soft fur, and caress their round
ears and the sensitive corners under their ears, and play with
them, and, it's as though, they are *welcoming* me home. Oh
look! A tall, fair girl...she's coming my way. Smiling. She
gives me a kiss and takes my hand and leads me through
gardens to a great avenue of tall, dark trees and bronze statues
and friendly white doves. The girl speaks to me in such a
pleasant voice. We talk of many things.

(MONKEY NOISES)

Aha! *A monkey*! Wearing a yellow suit. He's joined us. Yes,
happy...*happy* times.

NARRATOR
"Well, he goes on and on...it's funny, he said he couldn't
describe the place, but, now, he remembers every detail. All
the wonderful architecture. Palaces. Fountains. Everything a
heart desires. And, people? All beautiful and kind. All glad to
see him with love in their eyes. They play games with him in
the soft green grass."

WALLACE
And, there comes another woman....a somber, dark woman
...with a grave, pale face and wearing a long purple robe,
carrying a book and taking me aside while my playmates call to
me. "Come back to us!" they say. Well, she takes me aside to a
gallery and shows me that book...and, I see myself within. A
story about me. All the things that have happened to me since
I was born. Not pictures...but, *moving* realities. Do you
understand?

NARRATOR

Not really. Like motion pictures?

WALLACE

Almost, *yes.* People moving about, time coming and going.
My *mother!* I had nearly forgotten how she looked. My father,
stern and upright. The servants, the nursery, all the familiar
things of home. Right up to the moment I am hovering and
hesitating outside the green door. What's next? I want to
know. The page turns...it is *not* the wonderful garden world
with the leopards I see. No, it shows a long gray street in the
city. Freezing cold. The lamps are lit. There's a wretched little
figure...weeping. *Me.* I hear their voices, "Come back to us!"
The harsh reality is, I am standing alone. Where have they
gone? It's *really* me, you see. I had run away and here I am,
standing here, a boy of five, lost. Soon, there's a crowd and
next a policeman and, soon, I am returned home. I tried to tell
everyone about the door, but, my father gave me a *beating* for
telling lies. Later, I told my aunt, but, she punished me for my
wicked persistence. No one would listen to me. Even my fairy
tale books were taken away from me, because, I was...*too*
imaginative.

NARRATOR

Really?

WALLACE

Yes, they did that! So, I just whispered my story to my pillow
which was often soaked with tears. And, I prayed, *Please God.
Make me dream of the garden. Oh! take me back to my garden!
Take me back to my garden!* I dreamt of it, again, but, could
not return to it. It's hard to remember. I was only five at the
time.

NARRATOR

Haven't you attempted to find that location all this time? It may
actually exist, no?

WALLACE

Well, I was watched over most of my young life after my escape
at age five. No, it wasn't until *you* knew me that I tried for the
garden again. And, I believe there was a period...incredible as

it seems now...when I forgot the garden, altogether...when I was about eight or nine it may have been. Do you remember me as a kid at grade school?

NARRATOR

Unfortunately, *yes!* But, I don't recall any signs of you having a *secret dream* back then.

WALLACE

I used to play a game with myself...wherein, I had to find a new passage to school every day...as if, I was an explorer, Lewis and Clark, The Northwest Passage, and all that.

NARRATOR

Nope. Don't recall that at all. Wait...I *do* recall you being late quite often. That explains it.

WALLACE

Well, one day, I'm off in some direction I hadn't gone before ...working my way through unfamiliar streets, down to the low class area, on the other side of Campden Hill?

NARRATOR

Oh, yeah.

WALLACE

And, it's getting later, and I'm realizing I am lost now. And I walk past a row of dirty, old shop windows and they look familiar to me and...I keep going and *behold!* The white wall!

NARRATOR

And, the green door?

WALLACE

Yes! Don't you see? It wasn't a dream...

NARRATOR

And...you went in?

WALLACE

Well...not exactly...the idea of getting to school was overwhelming to me. I didn't want to be marked tardy once

again. I'd have to face my father's anger. Besides, now that I
knew that the door existed...I'd memorize my way back to
school and return there later. So, I ran and ran and got to
school, breathless, in time.

                    NARRATOR
So, you *didn't* go through the green door? After all *that,* you
didn't...?

                    WALLACE
I suppose I thought it was great to know it's there, to know my
way back to it... but, I *had* to get to school that morning. I
couldn't keep my mind on schoolwork all day, naturally,
thinking about the beautiful, strange world and its people
awaiting me. Won't they be glad to see me?

                    NARRATOR
So, you returned there that day after school?

                    WALLACE
Well...no. I didn't go *that* day at all. The next day was a half-
day holiday. I told myself, I'll go then. I don't know. What I *do*
know is that, in the meantime, the enchanted garden was so
much upon my mind that I could not keep it to myself.

                    NARRATOR
Who did you tell?

                    WALLACE
What was his name? Looked like a ferret? Used to call him
ferret face?

                    NARRATOR
Gerard Hopkins.

                    WALLACE
Yes, Hopkins. I told him.

                    NARRATOR
Not *me?*

WALLACE

I did not *like* telling him, I had a feeling that in some way it was against the rules to tell him, but, I did. He was walking part of the way home with me, talking, talking...and, suddenly, I blurted it all out to him. Well, of course, he told my secret to everyone. The next day in the schoolyard, I found myself surrounded by half-a-dozen bigger boys, teasing me, all wanting to know more about my *enchanted* garden. You weren't there that day.

NARRATOR

I must have had the flu.

WALLACE

A boy is a creature of odd feelings. I was, I really believe, in spite of my secret self-disgust, a little *flattered* to have the attention of these big guys. There was that fat oaf, Crenshaw, *praising* me for making up such a great story. Of course, I felt shame, too. I mean, this was *my* secret, bestowed upon *me*... now, I'm using it to gain some notoriety. Know what I mean? It's as if I betrayed a great trust given to me. Meanwhile, the fools are making fun about it, joking about the girl in the garden...

NARRATOR

What do you do?

WALLACE

I pretend not to hear. They start to call me a liar. I tell them that I can *prove* it to them...I know where the door is. The green door. I can lead them there in ten minutes. Then, I change my mind, but, Crenshaw twists my arm until it turns blue. So, I lead the way. But...we never do find the white wall and the green door.

NARRATOR

Why not?

WALLACE

I just couldn't find it. And, afterwards...I looked for it, alone. I still couldn't find it.

NARRATOR

How did the big boys react?

WALLACE

Oh, well, they figured me for a liar, alright. Gave me a good beating with their fists. I remember sneaking home to hide my bruises. I cried myself to sleep, not from the beating, but, because, I was afraid I had lost my beautiful garden forever. In school, for the next whole term, it was the first time my grades fell off. I walked around in a daze.

NARRATOR

Oh yeah...that was the only time I won honors in mathematics that term.

WALLACE

I never saw the door again...until I was seventeen.

NARRATOR

Oh?

WALLACE

It leapt upon me for the third time...

(CAR ENGINE)

as I was driving to Boston on my way to Harvard. I had just one momentary glimpse. I was in my 1928 convertible, whizzing down a country road...my hair blowing in the wind...and, there it was...

(CAR SKIDS TO STOP, MOTOR PURRS)

I sit there a moment...wondering if I should reverse gears and...I don't even turn around in my seat to look at it...I do steal a glance at my rear view mirror...I feel, as if, I'm trying to get a peek at Medusa and, if I do, I'll turn to stone. I mean, I've got a scholarship to Harvard just ahead. My father was *ecstatic* over my receiving it. I'd never seen the man so happy, heaping praise, *rare praise*, upon me. If I stop now...I may miss that scholarship. *Harvard*. A whole career before me. Think, *think*. Can I *sacrifice* all that? Sure, the wonderful people behind that door were very sweet to me, very fine, but...maybe, I belong in *this* world, no? There's another door opening, you know? The door to my *career?*

(CAR IN GEAR, ROARS OFF)

Well...I have served that career. I have done...much work, much *hard* work. But, I have dreamt of the enchanted garden in a thousand dreams, and, seen its door, or, at least, *glimpsed* its door, four times since then.

NARRATOR

Four times?

WALLACE

Yes. For a while, as *this* world became bright and interesting for me... full of meaning and opportunity....the gentle charm of the garden became remote to me. Who wants to pat leopards and smell flowers, when I can dine with pretty women and distinguished, powerful men? I am rising quickly in the ranks of those people. But, not everything is so perfect.

NARRATOR

You could have fooled me.

WALLACE

Twice, I have been in love...I won't dwell on that. But, once...I went to someone who...she didn't think that *I* would come to *her.* And, what do you know? On the way to her, a bridge had collapsed, so, I was detoured onto a lonely road and...

NARRATOR

It happens again! The white wall and the green door? But, now, you're in Boston, not where you had seen it last, right?

WALLACE

Yes. It *is* odd. But, there it is. And, do you know what? I go on by. I have something more important to me, now. The door has no appeal to me today. Alright, maybe a bit. A momentary impulse to try the door. I'm a few yards away from it. I can peek in...wave to the leopards, at least. But, I *can't*...the lady is waiting for me. I drive on, once again. Years of hard work after that and never a sight of the door. It's only recently it has come back to me. With it, there has come a sense as though some stain has spread itself over my world. I begin to think of it as a sorrowful and bitter thing that I should *never* see that door again. Perhaps, I am suffering a little from overwork... perhaps, it's the onset of middle age.

NARRATOR

I know how *that* feels.

WALLACE

The brightness that makes effort easy has gone out of things recently... just now with all these new political developments ...I ought to be working. Odd, isn't it? But, I don't have it in me anymore. What *good* does it do? Is there *any* reward for all this? If so, it's a cheap reward. And, so, I now wish for that garden more than ever before. In the past, I've thrown away all that the door offers. I swear to myself, if *ever* I see it again...I *swear* that I will not hesitate...I will go and never return. The world can have all the glitter and gold. The next time...the next time... And, then...

NARRATOR

What? It appeared again?

WALLACE

The next time...on the eve of the party's campaign announcement for me as President...I couldn't disappoint them. I had to be there, of course. I'm sitting in the back of the limousine taking me to the festivities when...there it is, again, on a side street...the white wall and green door. Shall I tell the driver to slow down? No, I don't. *I can't!*

NARRATOR

Of course, not.

WALLACE

The next time after that...my father, dying...I'm rushing to his bedside. I know, he was a mean sonuvabitch, but, he's my *father*, after all.

NARRATOR

You had to be there, Wallace.

WALLACE

But, the third time was…just a week ago. I must debate
Frobisher over the new bill passed in our state and how it
affects the country…he wants to have it retracted, of course.
Raising doubt amongst my followers. Our party leader begins
to hint that it may have been a mistake.

NARRATOR

The bill?

WALLACE

My candidacy.

NARRATOR

No!

WALLACE

So, I must face Frobisher with all guns blazing…I study every
detail of that bill, every possibility…and, here I am again…on
my way to face a crucial turning point in my life…and, there *it*
is again…in Washington D.C., no less…the white wall and
green door. Passing by it again…this time, on foot leaving a
restaurant, discussing my strategy with my councilors. And,
out of the corner of my eye…I see it as we pass by not *two feet*
from the door. Should I stop and bid good night to them?
What might happen if I go in? They're shooting questions at
me and I'm not listening. They'll think I've lost my sanity.
Suppose I *vanish* now! The headlines tomorrow will read,
Amazing disappearance of a prominent politician! And what
about the bill, if it should be retracted? All that I had worked
for, for the benefit of the people of my state? *Gone?*
Well…obviously…here I am. Here I am, before you, *now*. My
chance has gone from me. Three times, in one year, the door
has been offered…the door offers peace, delightful beauty
beyond dreaming, a kindness no man on Earth can know. And,
I have rejected it. It has gone…passed me by, forever…

NARRATOR

How do you know?

WALLACE

I know. I know. I am left now to work it out, to stick to the tasks that held me so strongly when my moments came. You say, I have success...this vulgar, tawdry, *irksome*, envied thing? Yes, I have it. If it was a walnut, I could crush it in my hand for all it's worth. This loss...it's destroying me. I have no inclination to keep working. My soul is full of regret. What would people think of me if they knew? A powerful, popular Senator, now, a strong candidate for the most powerful seat in the world? Wandering streets, *alone,* grieving, lamenting out loud...looking for a door, for a garden, for God's sakes!

(MUSIC)

NARRATOR

"I can still see, now, his pale face and that *fire* in his eyes. I recall his words, his tones, as I glance at this morning's headlines and articles covering his death. Everyone in the nation is talking about it. His body was found late last night...in a deep, subway excavation several blocks from his home. There's a large, wooden wall surrounding the work area with a small door cut into its side for the workmen to enter and exit. It must have been left unlocked and Wallace entered some time last night...Walking home from work as he had done often enough. I suppose, in the near darkness...under the pale electric street lights near the excavation...the wooden wall might have looked white. And, that door...left open...could he have mistaken it for...? But, it wasn't a *green* door. I'm not certain, but, how could it have been?

"Now, I begin to think that much of what Wallace had told me...was the product of hallucinations. Our minds can play terrible tricks on us. His was a brilliant mind...better than most. These visions...they had become like *religious* experiences to Wallace. They thoroughly convinced him that he had found this *other* world. On the other hand...I've become more of a believer, lately, in the supernatural...more superstitious, if you will, of signs and portents. Foolish of me? Maybe. It could be, that...well, at least, *half* of what Wallace had described *was* true. That wall and door offered him an outlet, a secret and peculiar passage of escape into another and, altogether, more beautiful world. At any rate, you will say, it *betrayed* him in the end. But, *did* it betray him? There, you touch the innermost mystery of these dreamers, these men of vision and the imagination. *We* see our world fair and common...that wall was nothing but a wooden barrier built around a pit. By our daylight standard, the man walked out of security into darkness, danger and death. But...did *he* see it like that? I wonder. Doesn't it make you wonder?"

THE TERROR OF THE TWINS
By Dan Bianchi
From A Story By Algernon Blackwood

Cast – 3m
Length – 20 min
Synopsis – Twins await their father's curse

NARRATOR

No one could have foreseen the depth and bitterness of Jasper Cartwright's disappointment when his twins were born. In the Cartwright family, going back hundreds of years, there is a legal will that could not be broken…or so, Jasper believed…in which, the *oldest* son must inherit the estate. Until then, the Cartwrights had been childless. Now, Jasper had *two*…Ernest born just a minute later than Edward. So deadly close. Poor Ernest. To be robbed of his heritage. His reward for having been born a Cartwright. If Jasper had had a daughter, he'd have accepted a more reasonable defeat.

Sorry to say, this frustration played upon Jasper's thoughts on a daily basis. Until he grew to hate the *eldest* twin, Edward. He loved him, as well, of course. Was that unnatural? To the outer world, Jasper Cartwright appeared to be a man of self-control, the picture of rationality. But, inwardly…who knew that suppressed *rage* and bitterness constantly preyed upon his mind? All he could think about was how Ernest might be cheated from the wealth and power inherited with the Cartwright name. It was, as if, *Edward* had *stolen* it from him. Eventually, the hatred spread to *both* sons…now, Jasper believed both of his twin sons were conspiring against him.

When Jasper began to exhibit behavior that worried his wife and family, they suggested he see a psychiatrist, or a clergyman. But, he didn't. No one guessed or, suspected correctly, what had bothered him to the extent that his entire demeanor had changed right before their eyes. The twins, themselves, *however*, knew it.

EDWARD

At twenty-one… we shall know *more* why Father hates us.

ERNEST

I don't *want* to know, Edward.

NARRATOR

As years passed, there had been too many violent outbursts
from Jasper. Irrational arguments, muttering to himself,
striking servants and, then, the twins…he had become a
walking time bomb and his household feared him. The twins
blamed themselves for their father's condition, yet, they still
did not know the *reason* behind his hatred. In their final visit to
the asylum, he told them at the door of his padded cell. "You
are not two, but, one. I still regard you as one," he said. "And,
at the coming of age…by God, you shall find it out! *I shall
return!*" A week later, Jasper Cartwright was dead of a cerebral
hemorrhage.

ERNEST

I knew he hated us, Edward. But, I never knew *why.*

EDWARD

At twenty-one…we shall know more.

ERNEST

Did you see the anger in his eyes? The way he bared his teeth
at us. It's as if, with his final words, he *cursed* us. Why did he
do that, Edward?

(MUSIC)

NARRATOR

That was five years ago. Now, on the morning of their twenty-
first birthday…the twins still share the same biting, *inner* terror,
just as they shared all other emotions of their life…intimately,
silently. You see, they still do *not* know about the will. All they
know is that their father's curse shall manifest itself on their
21st birthday. They are so *terrified,* they have even asked the
vicar to sit up with them until midnight.

ERNEST

After midnight, the day will be over…we will be free of the
curse, no?

NARRATOR

The vicar, Mr.Curtis, does not believe in such things as curses. "I do not think for one moment that God would permit such a thing," he said. "All spirits are in the hands of God and the *violent* ones more especially."

EDWARD

Even if Father does not come himself... he will...send... someone, or something...He's had years to prepare for today ...even from the other world *beyond* this one. We've both known it for a long time...by odd things that have happened, by our dreams, by nasty, little, *dark* hints of various kinds, and by these persistent attacks of terror that come from nowhere ...especially, of late. Haven't we, Ernest?

ERNEST

Lately, Father has renewed his violence against us. Tonight, it will be a regular assault upon our lives, or minds, or *souls!*

NARRATOR

Mr.Curtis, is, of course, astonished to hear such nonsense. But, he sees real fear in the eyes and voices of the twins. He tries to console them with a false understanding..."I've heard that strong personalities may possibly leave behind them forces that continue to act."

EDWARD

That's exactly what *we* feel. Though, nothing has actually happened, yet, you know, and it's a good many years now since...

ERNEST

Since he *cursed* us.

NARRATOR

Meanwhile, none of the family knows what is going on this night in the library. Everything has been planned secretly. The three men sit near the fireplace on this cold, autumn night. Two Cambridge undergrads and the Vicar reading the Book Of Job. Mr. Curtis drones on and on as the twins sink deeper into the soft, leather chairs. He does not want to deliver a sermon in fire and brimstone. Best to produce a calm atmosphere.

The hours pass rather slowly this way.

(CLOCK CHIMES)

What follows next is a distressing and *dreadful* occurrence happening without the slightest warning or preparation. There is no gradual *presentiment* of any horror... no strange blast of cold air... no dwindling of heat or light... no *shaking* of windows or mysterious *tapping* upon furniture. Without all that, the black trappings of terror falls upon the scene.

ERNEST
Edward? Are you asleep? (Yawns) Nothing's going to happen. The Vicar's good influence has prevented it. *Ha!* What superstitious asses we've been...haven't we, Mr. Curtis?

NARRATOR
Now, Mr. Curtis, dropping his Bible, looks hard at him under the lamp. For, in that second, there comes about a most abrupt and dreadful change... and, so swiftly, that, the clergyman is taken utterly by surprise and has no time to think. There has swooped down upon the quiet library an immense hushing silence, so *profound,* that the Vicar thinks he has gone deaf. Out of this enveloping stillness there rises a living and abominable Invasion....soft, motionless, *terrific.* It's as though vast engines, working at full speed and pressure have suddenly dropped down upon them...from nowhere.

ERNEST
Haven't we, Mr. Curtis?

NARRATOR
And, Mr. Curtis answers..."Because everything has already happened...even as you feared it would."

ERNEST
What? What are you talking about? Look...Eddie's sound asleep... sleeping like a pig in slop. Doesn't say much for your Bible reading, you know, sir! *Ha!*

NARRATOR
The clergyman turns to Edward...is he truly sleeping? It's so unnatural during this commotion. Doesn't he *hear* that noise?

Feel that oppressive force bearing *down* on them?   This
monstrous invasion…it has affected everything.
(WIND, CHAOTIC SCREAMS, HELLISH
VOICES, WHISPERS, LAUGHTER)

The very objects in the room alter incredibly, revealing,
suddenly, behind their normal exteriors, horrid little hearts of
darkness. It is truly amazing… this vile *metamorphosis.*
Books, chairs, pictures, all yield up their pleasant aspect
…mocking him now with laughter, from their inner soul of
blackness…their *decay.* Yet, Ernest…just yawns and talks
lightly and chuckles…still noticing *nothing!* All this happens in
ten seconds or less.
(SUDDEN SILENCE)

Now, Mr. Curtis hears the chilling words of Edward…

EDWARD (ECHO)

Even if Father does not come, himself, he will send
someone…or, *something*…

NARRATOR

Mr. Curtis understands…so, Jasper has done both…both sent
and come himself. That violent mind of his, released from its
spell of madness in the body… yet, *still* retaining the old
unbreakable *hatred*…it's now *directing* the terrible, unseen
assault. This silent room, so hushed and still, is super charged
to the brim. The horror of it seems to peel the very skin from
his back. And, while Ernest notices nothing, Edward *sleeps!*
The Vicar, feeling helpless, *alone*, against a Legion…pours out
a silent prayer to God above.
(CLOCK STRIKES)

ERNEST

Hooray! It's alright, don't you see? It's midnight and
nothing's happened. All of it, sheer nonsense! All this time.
What we need is a good, stiff whiskey!

NARRATOR

Mr. Curtis says nothing, but, watches the young man get up
from his chair. There is something…a *change*…in his voice,
his manner, *gestures*, the very way he walks over the thick

carpet to the door. Ernest seems less real, less *alive*, his voice sounds...small. He appears shriveled...something has made him shrink.

ERNEST
I'll be back in a minute. I am so glad to rid myself of that overwhelming feeling...you have *no* idea!

NARRATOR
As he leaves the room...the power that, only Mr. Curtis knows had engulfed them so mightily, follows Ernest. Almost at the same moment, Edward awakens.

EDWARD
Oh, oh, *oh!* But it hurts! *It hurts!* I can't hold you... leave me. It's breaking me apart...

NARRATOR
The clergyman springs to his feet, pleading, "What's wrong, Edward!"

NARRATOR
But, within the blink of an eye, everything has become normal once more... the room, as it was before, the horror gone. There is nothing he can do, or say, for there is no longer anything to put right, to defend, or, to attack.

EDWARD
Oh my...I needed that sleep! I feel...*great.* Refreshed.

NARRATOR
The Vicar stares at him, suspiciously..."Are you alright, Edward?"

EDWARD
Of course! I feel wonderful. I can't explain it...it's as if I'm *twice* the man, now. I have to admit, Sir, your Book Of Job had hypnotized me to sleep. But, that sleep...it's invigorated me beyond....beyond...By the way, where's Ernie?

NARRATOR
Mr. Curtis cannot turn away his piercing gaze. It's Edward's

tone...it conveys the most complete indifference...a complete lack of loving concern for his brother. Mr. Curtis tells him, "Gone away, I suppose...gone to bed, I mean, of course."

NARRATOR

A dreadful conviction overwhelms Mr. Curtis as he stands there, staring, his heart in his mouth...he is positive that Edward, too, has changed...not outwardly, but, inwardly. This is not Edward's personality. Edward has always been a sullen boy. Now, it's as if his mind, spirit, *soul* has... wonderfully *increased.* Yes, but...this visible increase is, *somehow,* terrible. Instinctively, Mr.Curtis shrinks back from him. *Why?* Why has this night turned his soul *dizzy* with a kind of nausea? Why does he feel he must now *strike* Edward where he stands? Why does he....?

(DISTANT SCREAM)

EDWARD

That sounds like Ernest!

NARRATOR

They find Ernest, or, what had been Ernest, crouching behind the table in the hall, weeping foolishly to himself. On his face lay blackness. The mouth is open, the jaw dropped... he dribbles hopelessly... and from the face has passed all signs of intelligence...of spirit.

(MUSIC)

For a few weeks, he lingers on, regaining no sign of spiritual or mental life before the poor body, hopelessly wrecked, releases what is left of him, from pure inertia...from complete and utter *loss* of vitality. And, the horrible thing...or, so, the distressed *family* believes...is that, during all these weeks, Edward has shown an indifference that has been singularly brutal and complete. He's rarely even gone to visit his twin...and only *once* spoke of him by name...

EDWARD

Ernie? Oh, but Ernie is much better and happier where he is...!

NARRATION

Now, at 26 years of age, *Edward* is the proper patriarch of the

Cartwright family…

EDWARD
As it *should* be.   I *am* the oldest son, after all.

_____

THE HORROR FROM THE MOUND
By Dan Bianchi
From A Story By Robert E. Howard

Cast – 2m
Length – 20 min
Synopsis – An ancient Indian gravesite harbors an evil demon

STEVE

"This goddamned land…nothing but scorched earth out here. Should have stuck to cattle ranching. I'm no farmer. That blizzard last winter *destroyed* all the budding fruit. The corn got ripped to shreds just as it was turning yellow…battered into the ground by those *goddamned* hailstorms. Now, after all that…the drought. And, if *that's* not enough, the cotton…which somehow survived all of that…got stripped overnight by a swarm of *grasshoppers*. Lucky I don't own the land, only renting, so, I won't be staying round here much longer. There goes Juan Lopez. Coming home from his farm next to mine. Every night, coming home from the fields. And, every night when he passes that knoll, he *always* manages to go round it by sundown." Hey Juan! Wait a minute! Want to ask you something. It ain't none of my business, but, I just wanted to ask you…how come you always go so far around that old Indian mound?

JUAN

Non comprende.

STEVE

Oh, don't give me that. You know what I just asked you. You speak English good as me. What's the matter? You think that mound's *haunted* or something?

JUAN

It is not a good place, no bueno. Let hidden things rest.

STEVE

I reckon you're scared of ghosts. Shucks, if that *is* an Indian mound, them Indians been dead so long their ghosts should be plumb wore out by now.

It's just filled with moldering bones of chiefs and warriors of a lost race.

JUAN
Best not to disturb what is hidden in the earth.

STEVE
Damn! Me and some boys busted into one of them mounds over in the Palo Pinto country and dug up pieces of a *skeleton* with some Indian beads and flint arrowheads and the like. I kept some of the teeth a long time till I lost 'em, and I ain't *never* been haunted.

JUAN
Indians? Who spoke of Indians? There have been more than Indians in this country. In the old times strange things happened here. I have heard the tales of my people, handed down from generation to generation. And, my people were here *long* before yours, Senor Brill.

STEVE
Yeah, you're right. First white men in this country was Spaniards, of course. Coronado passed along not very far from here, I hear-tell. Fernando de Estrada's expedition came through here...I dunno how long ago.

JUAN
In 1545....They pitched camp where your corral stands now.

STEVE
How come *you* know so much about it?

JUAN
One of my ancestors marched with de Estrada. A soldier, Porfirio Lopez... he told his son of that expedition, and *he* told *his* son, and, so, down the family line to me, who have no son to whom I can tell the tale.

STEVE
I didn't know you were so well-connected. Maybe you know something about the *gold* de Estrada was supposed to have hid around here,

JUAN

There was no gold...De Estrada's soldiers bore only their weapons, and they fought their way through hostile country...many left their bones along the trail. Later, many years later...a mule train from Santa Fe was attacked by Comanches not many miles from here and they hid their gold and escaped... so, the legends got mixed up. But, even *their* gold is not there, now, because Gringo buffalo-hunters found it and dug it up.

STEVE

I guess out here, there are more tales of lost treasure than anywhere else in America.

JUAN

Just think of all the gold and silver that passed back and forth over the hills and plains of Texas and New Mexico in the old days... back when Spain owned the mines of the New World and controlled the rich fur trade. And, then, came the...

STEVE

Yeah, yeah... Well, anyway, I got nothing else to do, so, I'm thinking of digging into that old mound and see what I can find.

JUAN

Dios, no! Don't do that, Senor Brill! There is a *curse*...my grandfather told me...

STEVE

Told you what? (Pause) Told you *what?*

JUAN

I cannot speak...I am sworn to silence. But, believe me when I say... better for you to cut your throat than to break into that accursed mound.

STEVE

Well, if it's so bad, why don't you tell me about it? Give me a logical reason for *not* busting into it.

JUAN

I cannot speak! *I know!* But, I swore to silence on the Holy

Crucifix, just as every man of my family has sworn. It is a thing so dark, it is to risk damnation even to speak of it! Were I to tell you, I would blast the *soul* from your body. But, I have sworn...and, I have no son, so, my lips are sealed forever.

STEVE
Aw, well...why don't you just write it out? Just *write* it out...then, you won't be breaking no promise of talking about it...

JUAN
(Pause) I will! Dios be thanked the good priest taught me to write when I was a child. My oath said nothing of *writing*. I only swore not to speak. I will write out the whole thing for you, if you will swear not to speak of it, afterward, and to *destroy* the paper as soon as you have read it.

STEVE
Sure, sure.

JUAN
Bueno! I will go at once and write. Tomorrow, as I go to work, I will bring you the paper and you will understand why no one must open that accursed mound! Buenos noche, Senor Steve!

STEVE
Good night, Juan. (Pause) "Yeah...you do that. So, there's a *mystery* to that mound out there, huh? Sure, it's an Indian tomb ...or, is it? Maybe, that was just the story to keep diggers away from it. Sure, maybe, those ancestors of Juan, they've got family gold hidden in it. Curse, indeed! In fact, I don't need no approval from Juan. I'll not wait for tomorrow, neither. But, the sun will be going down real soon. If I start digging now, I probably won't find anything before dark. Well, I can work by lantern light. I've tried doing things the normal way, working the land, trying to grow crops...*that* didn't work. Maybe, I can finally get something worthwhile out of this goddamned land, after all.

(MUSIC, DIGGING)

"Phew! This is hard work...didn't think the mound was so big and deep. This soil is baked like a brick. *Phew!* Well, the sun's almost down. I'm beginning to believe this may be a real Indian tomb. Bits of charcoal here and there. They used to build fires burning for days...burning the dead. It could just be that the Spanish didn't bury anything here...but, the mound builders...they might have hid away their own treasures with the dead.

(PICK STRIKES METAL)

"Well! Will you listen to that! Here it is...here now...what is it? Sharp points...I know what that is! That, there, is a *spur* of some sort. Yeah, I'll bet that belonged to some Spaniard, after all. It's all rusted and corroded now, but, it might have been down here a few hundred years. I wonder what it's doing deep in an Indian burial mound? I must be down six, seven feet deep. Well, might as well keep digging. There should be a narrow chamber built of heavy stones in the middle down here. That should contain the bones of the chief...and there should be victims they sacrificed just above it. Well...let's keep at it.

(MUSIC, DIGGING, PICK STRIKES STONE)

"Glory be! *Glory be!* That's not dirt anymore, that's rock. Let me hold the lantern here...yep, that's a solid block of stone, alright. A man-made block... look at the way it's been hewn. I must have hit the death chamber. Well, the damned thing is blocking the entrance...how am I going to get through this now? Maybe, I can get the pick into the edge somewhere and pry it out? Can't see a thing down here...didn't even notice, it's night up there. Well, I'll just dig around the stone here...and...

(FAINT SCRATCHING)

"Shush! What's that? Sounds like something *behind* the rock, no? Listen....yeah, that's where it's coming from. *Snakes!* Damn, there could be a dozen big diamond back rattlers coiled up in there just waiting for me! And, here I am poking around in holes in the dark. And, *phew!* Smell that? Damn, that's foul. Must be coming out of the cracks around the rock. Could be reptiles. Or, it could be...the smell of death. Maybe, some deadly gas trapped in there for hundreds of years from all the dead bodies...I think I'll just get out of here for now and head back to the house.

(MUSIC, SCREEN DOOR OPENS)

"Dark in here. Let me just light a lamp…

(STRIKES MATCH)

"There now. Should I have something to eat now? Nah, I'm
too riled up about that mound out there. I wonder what Juan
will say when he sees I've dug into it? Who cares? It's on *my*
land, ain't it?   It could be that all the gold I'll ever need is just
a few hundred yards away from me. I can get out of this
godforsaken land and head back East and…so, then, what am I
doing back here *thinking* about it? I can't sleep, that's for sure.
Let's go!

(MUSIC)

"Well! Will you look at *that* now! The damned rock…it's been
moved, *pushed* right aside. There's a room, a chamber or
something down there. Dark as hell. Now, I wonder…? Ah,
must have been that dirty coyote, Juan Lopez…he's been
spying on me, watching me work and when I left for a while, he
jumped in and pried open that rock and grabbed whatever was
in there for himself. Well, I'll fix him! Here, now…*look there!*
Under the moonlight…is that *him* just running off through the
mesquite. Look at him go! That's odd.   I mean, I ain't never
seen old Juan move so fast before. Sure, getting his *find* back
to his shack fast as he can run. Well, whatever he found is as
much *mine* as his. I got this land leased and I done all the work
digging. A curse, *hell!* No wonder he told me that stuff.
Wanted me to leave it alone so he could get it himself. It's a
wonder he ain't dug it up long before this.

(DESERT NIGHT SOUNDS,
OWL, CRICKETS, WHIPPOORWILLS.
DISTANT COYOTE HOWLS,
FOOTSTEPS WALKING ON DIRT)

"Look at all them stars up there…and the moon looking down.
Sure, makes a man feel real lonely out here at night. But, God
knows, there could be anything waiting for me out here
…including Juan. I should have brought my gun. All I got is
this here pick axe. There's his shack, now. Light in the
window. Looks like he's home. Probably packing to make a
getaway, I reckon. Well, we'll just see about…

(DISTANT BLOOD CURDLING SCREAM)

"Good God! What the hell….? Was that Juan?
(FOOTSTEPS RUNNING)

"Maybe, some wandering thieves got in…murdering Juan for his loot! I'm coming, Juan. *Hold on!*
(MUSIC. POUNDS ON DOOR, RATTLES LOCK)

Juan! Open up! It's me, Steve! You in there?
(MUFFLED NOISE, FURNITURE MOVING)

Alright, Juan…here I come…
(DOOR CRASHES OPEN)

Juan? You in here? (Pause) Juan?
(STRIKES MATCH)

Juan! Oh my God! Juan…who did this to you, buddy? "Jesus…he's dead. Damn! Look at that face of his…mouth open, eyes popping out…like he seen *Satan* himself. Here now…open window…his killer must have gone out that way. Wait! Is *that* him…out there running along the top of the hill? Gone. Well, Juan…helluva way to die. How *did* you die, exactly? No wound I can see. No knife stabbing or club marks on ya. I didn't hear no shots. Just a little blood here… streaming down your neck…what's that? A couple of punctures…were you stabbed by a thin stilletto, Juan, right there in the neck, old man? No? Looks more like something *bit* you. Like something with *fangs.* But, they don't look deep enough to have killed you. Not much blood around here. I'd say…you died of *fright,* old man. Heart attack. What you got there in your hand? Paper. This here's the curse he was writing about for me. Scrawled in the old Mexican's handwriting. He must have been sitting at the table writing this and someone sneaked in the window and…but, in God's name, *who?* Now, I got to saddle my horse and ride into Coyote Wells to tell the Sheriff. I'll just take these papers with me and…hold on…I'm forgetting that there's some crazy murderer out there in the dark. You know, that there figure I seen running…it's bothering me. Something *wrong* about it. Didn't look quite *normal.* And, Juan's death, it don't look quite normal neither. And, it's dark as Hell out there. And, all I got to defend myself is this here pick axe.

(DISTANT HOWL, HORSE WHINNIES,
RIDING OFF)

"Jesus! What in God's name...? Run! Get out of here now!

(MUSIC, RUNNING)

"*My horse*! The corral's open! Someone stole my horse! That bastard killed old Juan and stole my horse. Might as well go in then. I hope that scoundrel don't come back tonight. If he does, *I'll* fix him.

(SCREEN DOOR CLOSES)

"Well, now what am I gonna do? Town is miles away. Suppose that devil comes back for me? Suppose he thinks I'm a *witness* to what he done?

(LOCKS DOOR)

"Where's my revolver? Ah...

(SPINS CYLINDER ON GUN)

"Fully loaded, my friend. I ain't some old, unarmed man you sneak up on in the dark. Hey, nearly forgot about those papers Juan wrote for me. Nothing else to do but wait for the sun to come up. Might as well read em.

(MUSIC)

"Hernando de Estrada and some forty soldiers ...all those years ago..."

JUAN (VO)

"Captain Hernando de Estrada, who dared the deserts of the Southwest when all was strange and unknown. And the priest, and young Pedro Zavilla, and Don Santiago de Valdez....who was a mysterious nobleman, the sole survivor taken from an abandoned ship in the Caribbean. He said all had died of plague and he had thrown the bodies overboard. So de Estrada had taken him aboard his ship on its way to the New World. The explorers faced terrific hardships...drought, thirst, floods, desert sandstorms. And, hostile Indians. But, the greatest horror came in another form...as they journeyed through the wild country, man by man fell dead...and no man knew the slayer. Fear and black suspicion ate at the heart of the expedition. The Captain knew not where to turn. But, this they all knew... among them was a fiend in human form.

"The men suspected each other. Some began to desert the expedition. That made it easier for the fiend. The few explorers left were lost, dazed and helpless. Any stragglers became prey for the monster. Anyone left alone became victims. And, on the throat of each was found the wounds of pointed fangs that bled the victim white... so, that the living knew with what manner of evil they had to deal. Men reeled through the wild, calling on the saints, or blaspheming in their terror, fighting against sleep, until they fell with exhaustion and, once asleep, they never awoke.

"Then, the priest was attacked, but, he fought off his fiendish assailant and lived long enough to gasp the demon's name to de Estrada. The slayer was the ship survivor, Don Santiago de Valdez....who was a *vampire*. Yes, an undead fiend, living on the blood of the living. Then, de Estrada remembered... a certain foul nobleman who had lurked, in the' mountains of Castile since the days of the Moors....feeding off the blood of helpless victims which lent him immortality. This nobleman had been driven out... none knew where he had fled. Was Don Santiago the same beast? The people of his ship...had they really died from plague? Or, by the fangs of the vampire?

"The Captain and the few men left in the expedition decided that Don Santiago must be destroyed. Now, it is well known that a vampire, like a great serpent, when well gorged, falls into a deep sleep and may be taken without peril. And, so, they found the vampire asleep in the woods. But, de Estrada was at a loss as to how to destroy it. How may the dead be slain?

"The men wanted to drive a stake through the fiend's heart and cut off his head, uttering the holy words that would crumble the long-dead body into dust... but, the priest was dead. And, suppose the monster might awaken? So...they took the sleeping Don Santiago, lifting him softly, and bore him to an old Indian mound near by. This they opened, taking forth the bones they found there, and they placed the vampire within and sealed up the mound and there he shall stay until Judgment Day.

"It is a place accursed... and I wish I had starved elsewhere before I came into this part of the country seeking work...for I have known of this mound with its terrible secret, ever since childhood... so, you see, Senor Brill, why you must not open the mound and wake the fiend..."

STEVE
"Hmmm...that's it...no more. Hard to believe, but...it can't be *true*, can it? An old legend, probably, made up by superstitious settlers. Then, why did I find that old Spanish spur in the mound? An undead monster...*really?* Existing all this time down in that tomb? Am I to believe that...? *No!* It's madness. Juan, that old varmint, Juan, *he's* the one who's mad. Plumb loco! *Vampires?* They ain't no such things as vampires! If so, then why didn't the thing get *me* first instead of going to Juan's house to get *him?* It don't make sense. Just a pipe dream...Just a...Just...
(SUDDEN MUSIC)

"*Aaaaaaahhh!* Lord in Heaven! That *face* at the window! Those eyes! Gone...gone now. Phew! The stench...the same as at the burial mound. He's out there, somewhere...that *thing*...it's hunting me now.
(SILENCE. DOOR CREAKS)

"Damn, I'm trembling so much I can't aim this thing...
(COCKS GUN)

"Come on in, if you're coming, you...
(DOOR BURSTS OPEN)

"So, that there is a vampire, is it? Looks like a vulture to me. Icy eyes, long black fingernails. Stinks to high heaven. Moldering clothes from some other time. Is that a hat there with a crumbling *feather* on it? Why are you just standing there in the doorway? Brrr...it's cold all of a sudden. That thing...it brings the cold with it.
(VAMPIRE GROWLS)

"Oh damn, it's getting ready to…"

(GUNSHOTS)

Stay down, you thing from hell! I'll pump more lead into you if you want! "Damn…it's getting back up again!" *Aaaahhhhh!*

(FURNITURE CRASH)

Get your moldy claws off me!

(LONG FIGHT NOISE, SCREAMS, GLASS CRASH, FLAMES CRACKLING)

"Fire! The place is on fire! If I can only…those damned claws of his, digging into me…don't look into his eyes, man, don't….

(VAMPIRE GROWLS)

"This is it…he's getting ready for the kill…stalking me, playing with me like a cat and mouse…Doesn't he even *notice* the flames? The whole damned place is going up in flames! If I can just…get to the broken chair…and get me…

(VAMPIRE GROWLS, ATTACKS, SCREAMS)

Take that, you goddamned devil! Go on and scream! Scream like you never have before! Yeah, you don't like that there wooden chair leg jammed into your chest! You probably got no heart to speak of. Not dead yet, huh? Still looking at me with those flaming eyes, huh? Wriggling around like a snake on the floor…

(FLAMES CRACKLING)

I wish I can stay and watch you burn to dust, Don Santiago… comprende? But, I'm gonna go outside now…and watch these flames sail high as Heaven and pray all the time and when it's good and done…I'm gonna come in here and get your ashes and spread them in the wind…and *that* will be the end of you… once and for all….

(SCREEN DOOR SLAMS)

"Well, there's nothing left here to keep me now. I ain't got no treasure, nor money from the crops, but, I think I'll be heading back East now…back to the big city…maybe, Chicago or Kansas City…somewhere nice and safe where there's a lot of human beings… *normal* folk…some place where a goddamned vampire wouldn't stand a chance."

THE BEAST WITH FIVE FINGERS
By Dan Bianchi
From A Story By W.F.Harvey

Cast – 3m
Length – 25 min
Synopsis – A man's severed hand returns for revenge

NARRATOR

My story, I suppose, begins with Adrian Borlinger, whom I met when I was a little boy and he an old man. My father, who was a lodge brother of his, had taken me to visit him and before we left, Mr. Borlinger laid his right hand in blessing on my head. I shall never forget the awe in which I gazed up at his face and realized for the first time that eyes might be dark and beautiful and shining and, yet, not able to see. Adrian Borlinger was blind. But, he wasn't *always* blind.

He was an extraordinary man, who came of an eccentric stock. The Borlingers had sired champions of causes, patrons of science, founders of *weird* religions. Adrian was an authority on the fertilization of orchids. He was also a religious speaker who gave inspiring sermons and used his hands to heal.

All his life, Adrian Borlinger was exceedingly clever with his hands. His penmanship was exquisite. He illustrated all his scientific papers, made his own woodcuts, and carved sculptures.

When he was fifty-years old, Adrian lost his sight. But, he adapted quickly and learned to read Braille. He was still able to maintain an interest in botany. He could identify a flower by passing his long supple fingers over it. Towards the close of his life, he was credited with powers of touch that seemed almost uncanny. It has been said that he could tell the *color* of a ribbon placed between his fingers.

Adrian Borlinger was a bachelor. His elder brother, Charles, had married late in life, leaving one son, Eustace, who lived in the gloomy New England mansion, where he could work, undisturbed, in collecting material for his great book on heredity. Like his uncle, Eustace was a remarkable man. He lived alone with Saunders, his secretary whose business abilities were invaluable to Eustace.

Two years before his death, the old man developed the power of automatic writing. He'd sit, reading in bed, his forefinger of his left hand tracing the Braille characters, when a pencil held in his right hand would move slowly along the opposite page.

ADRIAN
Adrian Borlinger, Eustace Borlinger, Charles Borlinger, Francis Borlinger, Sigismund Borlinger, Adrian Borlinger, Eustace Borlinger, Saville Borlinger. B for Borlinger. Honesty is the Best Policy. Beautiful Belinda Borlinger. King George ascended the throne in 1760. Crowd, a noun of multitude, a collection of individuals. Adrian Borlinger, Eustace Borlinger.

NARRATOR
Nearly every page was scored with a meaningless jumble of capital letters, short words, long words, *incomplete* sentences. Now, his nephew Eustace caught wind of this and studied the pages. He was most interested in his uncle's new found ability. Again, he put the pencil in Adrian's hand...and read off every word as they were written...

EUSTACE
"Blundering Borlingers, unnecessarily unnatural, *extraordinarily* eccentric, culpably curious."

NARRATOR
Then, he'd question his uncle...who would reply as if with another voice...

EUSTACE
What the hell does *that* mean? Who *are* you? Is it my uncle who is writing? Is it anyone I know?

ADRIAN
Silly Eustace...you'll see me very soon?

EUSTACE

When shall I see you?

ADRIAN

When poor old Adrian's… dead.

EUSTACE

Where shall I see you? "

ADRIAN

Where… shall you not? What is the time?

EUSTACE

Ten minutes before four.

NARRATOR

Then, old Adrian suddenly wrote at a feverish pace. Eustace waited until he had finished and then clutched the paper away to read it.

EUSTACE

"Put your book away, Eustace. Adrian mustn't find us working at this sort of thing. He doesn't know what to make of it, and I won't have poor old Adrian disturbed…. It's too late for Adrian, but, you and I are friends already, aren't we, Eustace Borlinger? Au revoir!"

NARRATOR

At that moment, Adrian Borlinger awoke quite startled.

ADRIAN

I've been dreaming again, strange dreams of dark cities and forgotten towns. *You* were mixed up in this one, Eustace, though I can't remember how. Eustace, I want to warn you. Don't walk in doubtful paths. Choose your friends well.

(COUGHS)

EUSTACE

Don't excite yourself. I'll light the gas and ring for tea.

ADRIAN

I don't want you to be like me, Eustace. My whole life…wasted.

Such a failure.

EUSTACE
Nonsense, uncle, you're going to get well again. You've learned to use your hands better than any man with sight. Everyone says so. You're an inspiration...and just look at the possibilities of education in your field.

ADRIAN
Education is good so long as you know to whom and for what purpose you give it. Well, goodbye, Eustace...I may not see you again. You are a true Borlinger, with all the Borlinger faults. Marry, Eustace. Marry some good, sensible girl. Remember, my will is at my solicitor's. I know you're well provided for...but, I thought you might like to have my books. Goodbye!

EUSTACE
Why, uncle, I shall see you alive and well for many long years to come.

(MUSIC)

NARRATOR
Two months later Adrian Borlinger died. Eustace Borlinger was in Naples at the time. He read the obituary-notice in the Morning Post.

EUSTACE
Poor old fellow! I wonder if I shall find room for all his books. He's got enough to fill a library. Saunders will have his work cut out for him.

NARRATOR
When he returned home, Eustace found a mountain of correspondence waiting for him...and a curious wooden box that moved and rattled about his desk.

EUSTACE
Saunders! What the hell is that noise in there? It's kicking up a row, whatever it is. It's a box with holes in it...for breathing I suppose. Must be some kind of animal. A rat? Oh yes, we asked Morton to send us one for experimentation, no? We'll

need a cage for it.

(CRASH)

What's that? *Damn!* The box fell and now it's broken! The beast has gotten out. It's around here somewhere. It can get lost forever amidst all these cartons of books.

(CLICK)

Saunders! The lights just went out! Listen, there it is...it's at the other end of the room! It's gone into the gallery. Good.

NARRATOR
Then, he turned the lights back on and stood on a chair.

EUSTACE
I can't see a damned thing. Still too dark in here.

(CRASH)

It's in the other room now! Very well. You'll starve for this, my beauty! You'll have to come out sometime. *Me?* I'm just going to sit here and read my mail. Let's see....what's this?

NARRATOR
In a letter from the solicitor for the estate...Adrian had left *strict* instructions, that, there was to be *no* funeral and he was to be embalmed.

EUSTACE
"...but, with orders that his right *hand* should be sent to you stating that it was at your special request?" *My* special request? This is crazy...there must be some mistake...

(CRASH)

And what is that now? Ah, little fellow...you're playing with the window blinds and they came crashing down on you? Good. I can wait. Now, as for this request...I'll have to get to the bottom of it right away. My uncle was strange, but, this takes the ...*Aaagghhhh!*

NARRATOR
There...about ten yards in front of him...*crawling* along the floor...was no rat. It was, without a doubt...*a man's hand!*

Eustace stared at it in utter amazement. It was moving quickly like a caterpillar, or crab. Then, it disappeared around a corner. Pushing its way through books on the shelves, among the boxes. He tried to capture it with an empty box, to no avail.

EUSTACE
Saunders! Where are you? That beast in the box got out and I've been chasing it all over the place. Don't want it to start clawing at the books and ruining them.

NARRATOR
He didn't want to tell Saunders the real truth, not yet. Let *him* do the dirty work.

EUSTACE
Now, Saunders…I've got it cornered behind these books. You've got to help me to catch it. I'm not fooling you. It's right under that box. I need you to put your hand in there and get it.

NARRATOR
Well, he let his secretary attempt to capture what he thought was a lab rat…

EUSTACE
Watch out…it moves pretty fast.
(SAUNDERS SCREAMS)

Yes, I know…it feels like a hand. That's because it *is* a hand. With fingers and a thumb. Now, let's get it back in the wooden box and screw it down tight.

NARRATOR
Well, they did just that. And, then sat up all night staring at the box. At dawn, they opened the box again.

EUSTACE
Well, if *you're* not going to touch it, I will. Okay…here goes …ah. Well, it's not *so* cold as I thought it might be. Soft and supple too. If it's the embalming, it's a sort of embalming I've never seen before. I suppose it *is* my Uncle's hand alright. Let's put it back in the box and try to forget about it.

NARRATOR

But, the box was not as strong as they had hoped and, by dawn, the hand was on the loose again.

(FEMALE SCREAM)

By nightfall, the servants had quit.

EUSTACE

Idiots! They think the place is haunted. I've tried to offer raises, but, they won't take it. Strange noises, they say. One of them caught sight of something moving in the hall shadows. The bells ring at odd times, but, nobody is there. The blinds are drawn and opened. Some of them swore it was a *monkey* running wild in the house. Then, one of the maids...said she even *stepped* on it, tried to squash it...brave girl. Actually, she thought it was some kind of white *toad*. Brave, but, not *too* smart. They said they received notes...handwritten notes ...telling them to leave. So...*now*, the hand is writing notes, too. I should have *known* that might happen. It must have written that request to the solicitor bequeathing itself to me. Automatic writing. On the other hand, a lot of those notes, those *words* of his, were very odd, hardly the words of my uncle. Perhaps, the hand....is *not* him. I mean to say, perhaps, it is *possessed* by another spirit? In any case, we need to catch it.

(MUSIC)

NARRATOR

Three days later Eustace, writing alone in the library at night, saw it sitting on an open book at the other end of the room. The fingers crept over the page, as if it were reading...but, before he had time to get up from his seat, it scurried off and was pulling itself up the curtains out of reach.

EUSTACE

I know what I'll do, if I can only get it into the open, I'll set the dogs on to it. Do you *hear* me? *Can* you hear me? I've got two terriers that *love* to chase rats.

NARRATOR

So, he brought the terriers inside the house and all they managed to do was to tear up his slippers. Until one night...

(BARKING)

EUSTACE

Aha! *Saunders!* I think the dogs got it cornered!

NARRATOR

The dogs had indeed trapped the hand into a corner, but, were unable to get at it. Finally, when Eustace reached in and grabbed it, he noticed that there was a ragged gash across its back. Apparently, it had fought off the dogs. But, no blood oozed from the wound.

EUSTACE

Look at the fingernails, they've grown long and discolored. I'll burn the damned thing in the fireplace.

NARRATOR

But, he could not burn it. He tried to throw it into the flames, but, his own hands would not let him. And, so, Saunders found Eustace, pale and indecisive, with the hand still clasped tightly in his fingers.

EUSTACE

Saunders! Get me those nails and that hammer and a board of some sort. Don't worry, I've got it. The thing's quite limp... tired out from battling the dogs. Good...bring the hammer and board over there by the light. We'll make *sure* this thing doesn't take off again. We'll drive a nail through it, first, so that it can't get away. Then, we can take our time examining it. What are *you* scared about? You don't mind doing it to guinea pigs. Yes, I *know* that we don't fear revenge from guinea pigs, but, you're acting like an old lady. Just put the board down there and I'll hold it, spread it out for you...got the nail? Center it right there. Good...*now*...!

(HAMMER)

Look at it now. Writhing in agonized contortions, squirming and *wriggling* upon the nail like a worm upon the hook. At least, it can't scream. Where are you going, Saunders? Cover it up, man...cover it up! Put a cloth over it! *Here!* Now, lock it in the safe. That should do it. We'll keep it there till it dies...May I burn in hell, if I ever open the door of that safe again.

(MUSIC)

NARRATOR
Time passed. New servants were hired. Eustace did not follow the advice of his uncle and marry. He returned to old habits, attending parties and socializing. Then, came the burglary. The men, it was said, broke into the house by way of the conservatory. They only succeeded in carrying away a few pieces of Chinese pottery and a painting or two. But…the *safe* in the study was found open and empty. Eustace informed the police, he had kept nothing of value in it during the last six months. The police considered him a lucky man.

EUSTACE
The police say they will be able to trace the men. Professional thieves, they surmised. The way they got in and opened the safe shows that. But there's one little thing that puzzled them. One of the thieves, so they believed, was careless enough *not* to wear gloves. They traced his finger marks on the window sills in every one of the downstairs rooms. They were very distinctive ones, too. A right hand, every time. Also, they found this note…

ADRIAN (ECHOES)
"I've got out, Eustace Borlinger, but, I'll be back before long."

EUSTACE
No, Inspector…It's not the writing of anyone I know.

NARRATOR
As soon as the detectives left, Eustace made up his mind.

EUSTACE
Saunders, I'm not going to stay here any longer. Everything's been fine up until now.   I'm not going to run the risk of seeing that *thing* again. Get packed. Fill up the car. We're heading upstate to the cabin. We're getting out of here.

(MUSIC)

NARRATOR
The cabin was a six-bedroom family heirloom left to him by his

father. It was rural, but, clean and spacious and it came with a full household, including a great cook. But, it was the dead of winter.

EUSTACE
It's going to take us all day to unpack. We'll be here for quite a while. Why are you shivering? You oughtn't to feel cold, Saunders...when you can afford to sport a great fur-lined coat like that. You know how to spend your money well, I see. Look at those gloves, for instance. Who could possibly feel cold when wearing them? Go ahead and put them on if you must...I think you're being ridiculous to wear them in the house.
(SAUNDERS SCREAM)

NARRATOR
The glove was crawling across the bed.

EUSTACE
It's the hand! Get it! It's come along with us, after all...do you have it? Throw it in the bathroom! *Go ahead!* Good... good...it's hit the wall and fallen into the bath. Get that lamp ...let's have a look.

NARRATOR
There it was, old and maimed, dumb and blind, with a ragged hole in the middle, crawling, *staggering*, trying to *creep* up the slippery sides, only to fall back, helpless.

EUSTACE
Stay in there, you son of a....Saunders, I'll empty a suit case and we'll jam it in and throw it in the middle of the lake. That's what we'll do. Damn! It's getting out now...look at it, it's climbing up the plug-chain. No, you don't, you filthy...Come back, Saunders...it's getting away from me. I can't hold it! It's all slippery. And, its claws are digging into me! *Owww!* Shut the window, you idiot! Oh no...It's got out!

NARRATOR
The hand escaped and fell down onto the concrete walkway below. Eustace could hear the dull thud. He fainted and, for the next week, he became very ill. The doctor assumed that he had suffered from a great emotional shock.

(DOOR CLOSE)

EUSTACE

Doctors! If only they knew! Saunders, I don't want anyone else here. They'd smuggle it in, somehow. I know they would. This sort of thing can't go on, indefinitely. *You* saw it. It was half dead. Or *all* dead. Whatever. It can't go on living much longer, especially after that fall out the window. Every bone in it must be broken. As soon as I'm a bit stronger, we'll leave this place, no baggage, but, with only the clothes on our back, so, that, it won't be *able* to hide anywhere. We'll escape that way. We won't give any address, and, we won't have any parcels sent after us. I'll be well enough to leave in a day or two. That *has* to work. What have *I* done? Why does it come after *me?* I'm no worse than other men. I'm no worse than *you,* Saunders, you know I'm not. Before we caught the hand in the library, it was filled with *pure* malevolence...to me and all mankind. After we spiked it through with that nail, it naturally forgot about other people and concentrated its attention on *me.* It was shut up in that safe, you know, for nearly six months. That gives plenty of time for thinking of revenge. Thinking? Does it even *think?*

(THUNDER)

NARRATOR

The evening of October 31 was cold and rainy. The servants had taken out most of the furniture and curtains in Eustace's room so, that, it was almost bare. The staff just figured their boss disliked dirt, so much, he needed to see into all the corners of the room. But, when he asked for the windows to be *nailed* shut...

EUSTACE

Have they done all I asked? Good. Saunders, that note was just left at the front door. What is it? Give it to me. Hmm, no address nor signature. "Will eleven o'clock tonight be suitable for our last appointment?" Who is it from? Nevermind, I can guess.

(CLOCK STRIKES ELEVEN)

Listen...

(KNOCKING)

It's here, Saunders! Is the door bolted? Good. Now, Saunders, let's have a drink and a cigar. We won't let that *thing* out there interfere with …

(TAPPING)

What's that? The wind? Blowing against the shutters, I suppose. *Look!* It's at the window! What's it holding? A pocket knife. It's going to try to open the window with the blade. Well, let it try. They can't be opened that way. *Ha!* Saunders, pour me a whiskey. There's nothing supernatural about that hand, Saunders. I mean, it seems to be governed by the laws of time and space. It's not the sort of thing that vanishes into thin air or slides through oaken doors. And, since that's so, I *defy* it to get in here. We'll leave the place in the morning. I, for one, am *through* with being frightened by it. Fill your glass, man! The windows are all nailed shut. The door is locked and bolted. Drink, man! What are you waiting for? *What?* What do you mean it can still get in? The fireplace? The chimney? We've forgotten…? *Quick!* Light the fire, man! Give me a match, quick! The matches? Where are they? Hurry, get them out! Got one?

(STRIKES MATCH)

Good. And, throw some of that oil from the lamp onto the wood. And, toss in the bed sheets. Get it roaring hot…look out, man!

NARRATOR
Saunders was a little too hasty with pouring the oil from the lamp. The bed sheets had exploded into flames which were leaping out at them across the wooden floor.

(FIRE CRACKLING)

EUSTACE
You've set the place on fire! Try beating it out with a blanket! It's no good! It's not working. Open the door, Saunders, and get help.

NARRATOR
Saunders ran to the door and fumbled with the bolts. The key was stiff in the lock.

EUSTACE

Hurry, it's spreading to the bed!

NARRATOR

The key turned in the lock, at last. For half a second, Saunders stopped to look back. Afterwards, he could never be quite sure as to what he had seen, but, at the time, he thought that something black and *charred* was creeping slowly, *very slowly*, from the mass of flames towards Eustace Borlinger. For a moment, he thought of returning to his employer...but, the noise and the smell of the burning sent him running down the passage, crying for help. He rushed to the telephone to call for aid, then...

(EUSTACE SCREAMS, MUSIC)

Years later...this is the story which was told to me by my fellow math teacher at the local high school, Mr. Saunders. One day, I had mentioned, by chance, the name of Adrian Borlinger, and *that's* when he began to tell me this tale. He didn't tell me the *whole* story, all at once. I've had to piece it together. Apparently, he blamed *himself* for the tragedy that killed Eustace Borlinger.

As for the five fingered beast...he thought that it was animated, not by old Adrian, but, by the spirit of Sigismund Borlinger, a sinister eighteenth-century ancestor, who, according to legend, worshipped Satan. Why he cursed the last of the Borlingers to die a terrible death, I have no idea. Naturally, there's no clear cut proof of Mr. Saunders's story. All the letters were destroyed, as was the hand, itself. Or, so,, Mr. Saunders had assumed. But, for the rest of his life....whenever he heard the smallest of sounds, a branch tapping at the window, or, the scurrying of leaves in the wind, or, if something should suddenly drop...

(SAUNDERS SCREAM)

THE MOST DANGEROUS GAME
By Dan Bianchi
From A Story By Richard Connell

Cast – 3m
Length – 40 min
Synopsis – A shipwrecked man is hunted by an insane nobleman

(MUSIC, ENGINE, SHIP HORN,
WAVES AGAINST BOAT)

WHITNEY
Off there to the right…somewhere…is a large island.   It's rather a mystery,

RAINSFORD
What island is it?

WHITNEY
The old charts call it Ship-Trap Island. A suggestive name, isn't it? Sailors have a curious dread of the place. I don't know why. Some superstition.

RAINSFORD
Can't see it.

WHITNEY
You've good eyes and I've seen you pick off a moose moving in the brown fall bush at four-hundred yards, but,even *you* can't see four miles or so through a moonless Caribbean night.

RAINSFORD
Nor four yards. *Ugh!* It's like moist black velvet out there.

WHITNEY
It will be light enough in Rio. We should make it in a few days. I hope the jaguar guns have come from Purdey's. We should have some good hunting up the Amazon. Great sport, hunting.

RAINSFORD
The best sport in the world.

WHITNEY

For the hunter. Not for the jaguar.

RAINSFORD

Don't be ridiculous, Whitney. You're a big-game hunter, not a philosopher. Who cares how a jaguar feels?

WHITNEY

Perhaps, the jaguar does.

RAINSFORD

Bah! They've no understanding.

WHITNEY

Even so, I rather think they understand one thing...fear. The fear of pain and the fear of death.

RAINSFORD

Nonsense, This hot weather is making you soft, Whitney. Be a realist. The world is made up of two classes...the hunters and the huntees. Luckily, you and I are hunters.

WHITNEY

Do you think we've passed that island, yet?

RAINSFORD

I can't tell in the dark.

WHITNEY

I hope so.

RAINSFORD

Why?

WHITNEY

The place has a reputation...a bad one.

RAINSFORD

Cannibals?

WHITNEY

Hardly. Even cannibals wouldn't live in such a God-forsaken

place. But, sailors have built up a legend about the place. Didn't you notice that the crew's nerves seemed a bit jumpy today?

RAINSFORD

They *were* a bit strange, now you mention it. Even Captain Nielsen.

WHITNEY

Yes, even that tough-minded old Swede, who'd go up to the devil himself and ask him for a light. Those fishy blue eyes held a look I never saw there before. All I could get out of him was "This place has an evil name among seafaring men, sir." Then he said to me, very gravely, "Don't you *feel* anything?"...as if the air about us was actually poisonous. Now, you mustn't laugh when I tell you this...I *did* feel something like a sudden chill. There was no breeze. The sea was as flat as a plate-glass window. We were drawing near the island, then. What I felt was a...a mental chill... a sort of sudden dread.

RAINSFORD

Pure imagination. One superstitious sailor can taint the whole ship's company with his fear.

WHITNEY

Maybe. But, sometimes I think sailors have an extra sense that tells them when they are in danger. Sometimes, I think evil is a tangible thing...with wave lengths, just as sound and light have. An evil place can, so to speak, *broadcast* vibrations of evil. Anyhow, I'm glad we're getting out of this zone. Well, I think I'll turn in now, Rainsford.

RAINSFORD

I'm not sleepy. I'm going to smoke another pipe up on the afterdeck.

WHITNEY

Good night, then, Rainsford. See you at breakfast.

RAINSFORD

Right. Good night, Whitney.
(ENGINES, MUSIC, SURF, SEA BIRDS)

"It's so dark, I could sleep without closing my eyes… the night will be my eyelids.

(DISTANT GUN SHOT)

"What's that?

(DISTANT GUN SHOTS)

"Gunfire! Out there in the darkness…the island. Can't see a damned thing. If I can just get up on this railing and look out over…my pipe! *Whoa!*

(SCREAMS, SPLASH)

(Drowning) *Help! Help!* Man…over…board!

(WAVES, SHIP ENGINE FADING)

"Gone…the boat's *gone!* Just like that. Nobody heard me. They're not stopping. What am I gonna do? Ok, ok…you're gonna swim for it. Maybe, they'll notice you're missing…nah, it's the middle of the night…they won't know until morning…I can barely see its lights anymore…it's not stopping. The gun shots! Yeah…ok …came from the island…maybe I can make it…gotta take it slow, conserve strength…maybe…

(ANIMAL HOWL, GUNSHOT)

"Listen! That's not too far. That was a pistol shot. You can make it to the island. Swim, boy, *swim*…sure hope there aren't any sharks around here…

(MUSIC, WAVES CRASHING)

"What? Waves…crashing onshore…you're gonna make it…watch out for the rocks, don't wanna come this far to get your brains smashed in…

(MUSIC, WAVES)

(Exhausted) Thank God! Made it…I made it…climb up on the rock, boy…you made it….ok, ok…rest awhile, take a look where you are…what do you see? I see…jungle…coming down to the beach…cliffs. High cliffs. Underbrush, dense. I've been through all that before. At least, I'm safe now. Gotta sleep. Sleep.

(MUSIC, SEA BIRDS)

"Oh…look at that morning sun! Never thought you'd see that again, huh, boy? (Stretches) *Oh!* My muscles are aching awful…but, thank God I've got muscles…anyone out of shape might have gone under within minutes. But, oh, I'm hungry now. So, where am I? You know…I completely forgot those gun shots. Where there are pistol shots, there are men. Where there are men, there is food. But, what kind of men? Who'd want to be here? No sign of any trails. Great. That means triple work fighting my way through all the vines and weeds. Maybe, it's easier if I just take the shoreline. Well…let's get going…

(MUSIC)

"This island can't be so big. Feels like I've been walking for a couple of hours…

(NOISE IN BUSH)

"Hold on! What's that? Sounds like something large. An animal… thrashing about in the high weeds…could be wounded. And, there are patches of blood. Aha! Here's an empty cartridge. A twenty-two. By the looks of the grass padded down here and the big patches of blood…it's a big animal. It's odd that the hunter only used a pistol. It's clear that the beast put up a fight. I suppose the first three shots I heard was when the hunter flushed his quarry and wounded it. The last shot was when he trailed it here and finished it. Yeah, those prints in the mud…hunting boots. Going toward the cliff where I'm heading. It's going to be dark pretty soon and I'll lose direction. Better get moving.

(MUSIC)

"Up there! Finally…*lights!* It'll take some climbing, but…lots of lights, maybe it's a village.

(MUSIC)

"Well…that's no village, after all. Looks like towers…one big building…a castle. On a high bluff overlooking a sharp drop down to the rock and sea. Well, can you beat that? What's *that* doing out here? I sure hope it isn't a mirage.

(MUSIC, IRON GATE)

"This castle looks like something out of a fairy tale…stone

steps, a moat, and that big wooden door with one of them gargoyles leering at you as a door knocker. Well, might as well see if it works.

(DOOR KNOCKS, ECHO)

"No one home. Maybe, there's a back entrance...I'll go this way...

(DOOR OPENS, CREAKS)

"Yow! He's a *big* fella. As big as a bear. And, he's holding a .45 and pointing it straight at me." Don't be alarmed, I'm no robber. I fell off a yacht. My name is Sam Rainsford of New York City. "He's just staring at me. Guess they don't get many visitors around here. Maybe, he doesn't understand English. He's dressed in a black uniform I don't recognize." I'm Sam Rainsford of New York. I fell off a yacht. I am hungry.

(COCKS PISTOL)

"Oh no...now what? He's turning, giving a military salute, clicking his heels together...someone's coming. Yes, down the marble staircase...well, it's a man dressed in evening clothes. Tall man, fifty ish...white hair. But thick eyebrows. Aristocratic."

ZAROFF

It is a very great pleasure and honor to welcome Mr. Sam Rainsford, the celebrated hunter, to my home. I've read your book about hunting snow leopards in Tibet, you see. I am General Zaroff.

RAINSFORD

How do you do?

ZAROFF

Ivan, put your pistol away. Ivan is an incredibly strong fellow, but, he has the misfortune to be deaf and dumb. A simple fellow, but, I'm afraid, like all of his race, a bit of a savage.

RAINSFORD

Is he Russian?

ZAROFF

He is a Cossack. So am I. Come, we shouldn't be chatting here. We can talk, later. Now, you want clothes, food, rest. You shall have them. This is a most restful spot. Follow Ivan, if you please, Mr. Rainsford. I was about to have my dinner when you came. I'll wait for you. You'll find that my clothes will fit you, I think.

(MUSIC)

RAINSFORD

Your home here is...remarkable, General Zaroff. Reminds me of mansions I've seen in Europe built for royalty. It has a medieval magnificence about it. My bed looks like something Queen Catherine might have slept in. And this food...a banquet fit for a King. Are there others here on the island? I ask, because, this table...you can sit twenty easily.

ZAROFF

You'll have a cocktail, Mr. Rainsford?

RAINSFORD

Yes, thanks. All of these animals...the mounted heads...lions, tigers, elephants, moose, bears...the stuffed exhibits. It's like a museum. Wonderful specimens. Hmm, this cocktail is delicious.

ZAROFF

Try the borsht...with the whipped sour cream.

RAINSFORD

Oh yes. And this filet mignon is simply marvelous. It appears that you live in the life of luxury, General. I'm envious.

ZAROFF

We do our best to preserve the amenities of civilization here. Please forgive any lapses. We are well off the beaten track, you know. Do you think the champagne has suffered from its long ocean trip?

RAINSFORD

Not in the least.

ZAROFF

Perhaps, you were surprised that I recognized your name. You
see, I read all books on hunting published in English, French,
and Russian. I have but one passion in my life, Mr. Rainsford,
and it is the hunt.

RAINSFORD

You have some wonderful heads here. That Cape buffalo is the
largest I've ever seen.

ZAROFF

Oh, that fellow. Yes, he was a monster.

RAINSFORD

Did he charge you?

ZAROFF

Hurled me against a tree. Fractured my skull. But, I got the
brute.

RAINSFORD

I've always thought that the Cape buffalo is the most
dangerous of all big game.

ZAROFF

Hmmm...well...No. You are wrong, sir. The Cape buffalo is *not*
the most dangerous big game. Here in my preserve on this
island, I hunt more *dangerous* game.

RAINSFORD

Is there big game on this island?

ZAROFF

The biggest.

RAINSFORD

Really?

ZAROFF

Oh, it isn't here naturally, of course. I have to stock the island.

RAINSFORD

What have you imported, general? Tigers?

ZAROFF

No. Hunting tigers ceased to interest me some years ago. I exhausted their possibilities, you see. No thrill left in tigers, no real danger. I live for danger, Mr. Rainsford. Cigarette?

RAINSFORD

Thanks. Hmm, smells like perfume.

ZAROFF

We will have some capital hunting, you and I. I shall be most glad to have your society.

RAINSFORD

But, what game...

ZAROFF

I'll tell you. You will be amused, I know. I think I may say, in all modesty, that, I have done a rare thing. I have invented a new sensation. May I pour you another glass of port?

RAINSFORD

Thank you, general.

ZAROFF

God makes some men poets. Some He makes kings, some beggars. Me, He made a hunter. My hand was made for the trigger, my father said. He was a very rich man with a quarter of a million acres in the Crimea, and, he was an ardent sportsman. When I was only five years old, he gave me a little gun, specially made in Moscow for me, to shoot sparrows with. When I shot some of his prize turkeys with it, he did not punish me... he complimented me on my marksmanship. I killed my first bear in the Caucasus when I was ten. My whole life has been one prolonged hunt. I went into the army...it was expected of noblemen's sons...and, for a time, commanded a division of Cossack cavalry, but, my real interest was always the hunt. I have hunted every kind of game in every land. It would be impossible for me to tell you how many animals I have killed. After the debacle in Russia, I left the country, for it was imprudent for an officer of the Czar to stay there. Many noble Russians lost everything. I, luckily, had invested heavily in American securities, so, I shall never have to open a tearoom in Monte Carlo or drive a taxi in Paris. Naturally, I continued to hunt...the grizzly bear in your Rockies, the crocodile in the Ganges, the rhinoceros in East Africa. It was in Africa that the Cape buffalo hit me and laid me up for six months. As soon as I recovered, I started for the Amazon to hunt jaguars, for I had heard they were unusually cunning. They weren't. They were no match at all for a hunter with his wits about him, and a high-powered rifle. I was bitterly disappointed. I was lying in my tent with a splitting headache one night... when a terrible thought pushed its way into my mind. Hunting was beginning to *bore* me! And hunting, remember, had been my life. I have heard that, in America, businessmen often go to pieces when they give up the business that has been their life.

                              RAINSFORD
Unfortunately...

                              ZAROFF
I had no wish to go to pieces. I must do something. Now, mine is an analytical mind, Mr. Rainsford. Doubtless that is why I enjoy the problems of the chase.

                              RAINSFORD
I understand, General Zaroff.

                              ZAROFF
So, I asked myself why the hunt no longer fascinated me. You are much younger than I am, Mr. Rainsford, and have not hunted as much, but, you, perhaps, can guess the answer.

                              RAINSFORD
What was it?

                              ZAROFF
Simply this... hunting had ceased to be what you call *a sporting proposition.* It had become *too* easy. I always got my quarry. *Always.* There is no greater bore than perfection. No animal had a chance with me anymore. That is no boast... it is a mathematical certainty. The animal had nothing but his legs

and his instinct. Instinct is no match for reason. When I thought of this... it was a tragic moment for me, I can tell you.

RAINSFORD

What are you saying, General?

ZAROFF

It came to me as an inspiration what I must do.

RAINSFORD

And, that was?

ZAROFF

I had to invent a new animal to hunt.

RAINSFORD

A *new* animal? You're joking.

ZAROFF

Not at all. I *never* joke about hunting. I needed a new animal. I found one. So, I bought this island, built this house, and, here I do my hunting. The island is perfect for my purposes...there are jungles with a maze of trails in them, hills, swamps...

RAINSFORD

But, the *animal*, General Zaroff?

ZAROFF

Oh, it supplies me with the most exciting hunting in the world. No other hunting compares with it for an instant. Every day I hunt, and I never grow bored, now, for I have a quarry with which I can match my wits.

RAINSFORD

I can't imagine...

ZAROFF

I wanted the ideal animal to hunt. So I said, "What are the attributes of an ideal quarry?" And, the answer was, of course, ...It must have courage, cunning, and, above all, it must be able to reason.

RAINSFORD

But, no animal can reason.

ZAROFF

My dear fellow, there is *one* that can.

RAINSFORD

But, you can't mean...?

ZAROFF

And, why not?

RAINSFORD

I can't believe you are serious, General Zaroff. You're playing with me.

ZAROFF

Why should I not be serious? I am speaking of hunting.

RAINSFORD

Hunting? But, General Zaroff, what *you* speak of is murder.

ZAROFF

(Laughs) I refuse to believe that so modern and civilized a young man as you seem to be harbors romantic ideas about the value of human life. Surely your experiences in the war...

RAINSFORD

Did not make me *condone* cold-blooded murder.

ZAROFF

(Laughs) How extraordinarily *droll* you are! One does not expect, nowadays, to find a young man of the educated class, even in America, with such a naive, and, if I may say so, mid-Victorian point of view. It's like finding a snuffbox in a limousine. Ah, well, doubtless you had Puritan ancestors. So many Americans appear to have had them. I'll wager you'll forget your notions when you go hunting with me. You've a genuine new thrill in store for you, Mr. Rainsford.

RAINSFORD

Thank you...I'm a hunter, *not* a murderer.

ZAROFF

Dear me. Again, that unpleasant word. But, I think I can show you that your scruples are quite ill founded.

RAINSFORD

Yes?

ZAROFF

Life is for the strong, to be lived by the strong, and, if needs be, *taken* by the strong. The weak of the world were put here to give the strong pleasure. *I* am strong. Why should I *not* use my gift? If I wish to hunt, why should I not? I hunt the scum of the Earth... sailors from tramp ships...lowlife scoundrels from prison ships... blacks, Chinese, Irish whites, mongrels...a thoroughbred horse or hound is worth more than a score of them.

RAINSFORD

But, they are *men!*

ZAROFF

Precisely, that is why I use them. It gives me pleasure. They can reason, after a fashion. So, they are dangerous.

RAINSFORD

But, where do you get them?

ZAROFF

This island is called Ship Trap. Sometimes, an angry god of the high seas sends them to me. Sometimes, when Providence is not so kind, I help Providence a bit. Come to the window with me. *Watch!* Out there! See the lights out there at sea?. On the buoys? They indicate a channel where there's none... giant rocks with razor edges crouch like a sea monster with wide-open jaws. They can crush a ship as easily as I crush this nut.
(CRACKS NUT)

Lights lure the men to this place. Yes, we have electricity. Why not use the benefits of modern civilization? We try to be civilized here.

RAINSFORD

Civilized? And ,you shoot down men?

ZAROFF

Dear me, what a righteous young man you are! I assure you, I do *not* do the thing you suggest. That would be barbarous. I treat these visitors with every consideration. They get plenty of good food and exercise. They get into splendid physical condition. You shall see for yourself tomorrow.

RAINSFORD

What do you mean?

ZAROFF

We'll visit my training school. It's in the cellar. I have about a dozen pupils down there now. They're from the Spanish bark San Lucar that had the bad luck to go on the rocks out there. A very inferior lot, I regret to say. Poor specimens and more accustomed to the deck than to the jungle. Hmm..this Turkish coffee is my favorite. You must have some.

RAINSFORD

I don't believe this...

ZAROFF

It's a game, you see? I suggest to one of them that we go hunting. I give him a supply of food and an excellent hunting knife. I give him three hours' start. I am to follow, armed only with a pistol of the smallest caliber and range. If my quarry eludes me for three whole days, he wins the game. If I find him... *he* loses.

RAINSFORD

Suppose he refuses to be hunted?

ZAROFF

Oh, I give him his option, of course. He need not play that game if he doesn't wish to. If he does not wish to hunt, I turn him over to Ivan. Ivan once had the honor of serving as official torturer to the Czar, and he has his own ideas of sport. Invariably, Mr. Rainsford, *invariably,* they choose the hunt.

RAINSFORD

And, if they win?

ZAROFF

To date I have not lost. I don't wish you to think me a braggart, Mr. Rainsford. Many of them afford only the most elementary sort of problem. Occasionally, I do find a challenge. One almost did win. I eventually had to use the dogs.

RAINSFORD

The dogs?

ZAROFF

Out this window here...do you see down there? The pen? It is dark, but, you can just make out those big dark shapes moving about...great danes. A dozen of them. A rather good lot, I think. They are let out at seven every night. You were lucky that you came here before then. If anyone should try to get into my house...or, out of it....something extremely regrettable would occur to him. And, now, I want to show you my new collection of heads. Will you come with me to the library?

RAINSFORD

I hope, that, you will excuse me tonight, General Zaroff. I'm really not feeling well.

ZAROFF

Ah, indeed? Well, I suppose that's only natural, after your long swim. You need a good, restful night's sleep. Tomorrow, you'll feel like a new man, I'll wager. Then, we'll hunt, eh? I've one rather promising prospect...Sorry you can't go with me tonight. I expect rather fair sport....a big, strong, black fellow. He looks resourceful...Well, good night, Mr. Rainsford. I hope you have a good night's rest.

(MUSIC)

RAINSFORD

"Walking the floor for hours. I've escaped the horrors of the sea for *this?* This waking nightmare? The man's a *maniac.* Pure and simple. Sure, he offers a nice meal, a luxurious bed ...still, who can sleep knowing what's going on out there at this very moment? I can't leave. If he's right about those mongrels

...and I'm sure he is...I wouldn't get ten feet away. Just *one* of them would tear me to shreds...but, *twelve* of them? Besides, the window's bolted shut. And, I'm forty feet up here in a tower. Look down there...the hounds know I'm here...I can see their green eyes staring up at me.

(DISTANT BARKING)

"There they go...can barely see their shadows...running off...I wonder why? Morning's almost here.

(DISTANT GUN SHOT)

"Oh, dear God!"

(MUSIC)

ZAROFF

Good morning, Mr.Rainsford. How are you? As for me, I do not feel so well. I am worried, Mr. Rainsford. Last night I detected traces of my old complaint. Ennui. *Boredom*. Ah, crepes Suzette! Have you had any? Oh, but, you must.

RAINSFORD

I'll stick to coffee, thank you.

ZAROFF

As you wish.   Now...The hunting was *not* good last night. The fellow lost his head. He made a straight trail that offered no problems at all. That's the trouble with these sailors... they have dull brains to begin with, and they do not know how to get about in the woods. They do excessively stupid and obvious things. It's most annoying.

RAINSFORD

General, I wish to leave this island at once.

ZAROFF

But, my dear fellow, you've only just come. You've had no hunting...

RAINSFORD

I wish to go today.

ZAROFF

(Pause) Hmmm....I *know!* Tonight, we will hunt...you and I.

RAINSFORD

No, General. I will not hunt.

ZAROFF

As you wish, my friend. The choice rests entirely with you. But, may I not venture to suggest that you will find my idea of sport more diverting than Ivan's?

RAINSFORD

You don't mean...?

ZAROFF

My dear fellow, have I *not* told you... I always mean what I say about hunting? This is really an inspiration. I drink to a true challenge worthy of my steel...at last. I salute you, Mr. Rainsford. You'll find this game worth playing. *Your* brain against mine. *Your* survival skills against mine. Your strength and stamina against mine. Outdoor chess! And the stake is not without value, eh?

RAINSFORD

And, if I win...?

ZAROFF

I'll cheerfully acknowledge myself defeated if I do not find you by midnight of the third day...My sloop will place you on the mainland near a town.

RAINSFORD

Oh...?

ZAROFF

Oh, you can trust me. I will give you my word as a gentleman and a sportsman. Of course, you, in turn, must agree to say nothing of your visit here.

RAINSFORD

I'll agree to nothing of the kind.

ZAROFF

Oh, in that case...But, why discuss that now? Three days
hence we can discuss it over a bottle of Chateau Lafitte,
unless...? Ivan will supply you with hunting clothes, food, a
knife. I suggest you wear moccasins... they leave a poorer trail.
I suggest, too, that you avoid the big swamp in the southeast
corner of the island. We call it Death Swamp. There's
quicksand there. One foolish fellow tried it. The deplorable part
of it was that Lazarus followed him. You can imagine my
feelings, Mr. Rainsford. I loved Lazarus...

RAINSFORD

Lazarus?

ZAROFF

He was the finest hound in my pack. Well, I must beg you to
excuse me, now. I always' take a siesta after lunch. You'll
hardly have time for a nap, I fear. You'll want to start, no doubt.
I shall not follow till dusk. Hunting at night is so much more
exciting than by day, don't you think? Au revoir, Mr. Rainsford,
au revoir.

(MUSIC, HACKING, JUNGLE SOUNDS)

RAINSFORD

"How long have I been on the run? Can barely see the sun
through these trees. Two...three hours? It's got to be a
hundred degrees. I wonder if he's already on my trail. No, he
said he leaves at dusk. He *said?* Who believes that mad man?
Keep your nerve, boy. Don't get careless. Make distance
between you and the castle. Keep going. Just don't panic.
Give him a false trail to follow...take him in loops...double
back. It works for the fox...well, some times.

(MUSIC)

"Exhausted. My legs...don't know how much more I can do.
My face and arms are cut to pieces by the branches. It's insane
to blunder on through the dark. Not that I'm strong enough to
do so. Well, you've played the fox, *now* you must play the cat.
See that big tree? Maybe, if you climb that tree and sit right up
there on that big limb...stretch out, stay low, like a leopard.
Yeah, even as great a hunter as General Zaroff won't see you
up there. Only the devil could follow that complicated trail

through the jungle after dark. On the other hand, the General just might be the devil...

(JUNGLE SOUNDS, MUSIC,
DISTANT THUNDER)

"Well...another night has passed on this cursed place. Not that I slept a wink. And rain on the way.

(BIRD CRY)

"Is he coming? Something is coming through the bush in that direction...Coming slowly, carefully, coming...Get down low, boy, and don't breathe. It's General Zaroff. So, he's made his way here...he's studying the ground, looking about. Right under the tree now...what if I should drop on him like a panther and ....ah, but, he's holding a pistol. He looks puzzled. What's he...? He's lighting a cigarette. He's blowing smoke rings. His eyes moving up the trunk of the tree...he's *smiling!* This is it, Rainsford, old boy. You're trapped like a rat...*wait!* He's walking away. Back along the trail he's come. There he goes! Look at me...shaking like a leaf. I'm sick and numb. That fiend could follow a trail at night. He must have supernatural powers. How had he *missed* seeing you? Why had the General smiled? Why had he turned back? He's playing with you! Cat and mouse. Saving you for another day's sport. Do not lose your nerve, old boy. Keep your head. What are you going to do? What? I've got it...I've got it...

(MUSIC)

"There now...finished at last. Now, all I have to do is wait... behind that fallen tree.

(MUSIC)

"Well...that didn't seem long. Here he comes...nothing escapes those searching eyes of his...no crushed blade of grass, no bent twig, no mark, no matter how faint, in the moss. Will he see the trap?   His foot, it's touching the branch, the trigger...

(TREE CRASH, MUSIC)

"It didn't work! *It didn't work!* He's been wounded in the shoulder, but, he's up, on guard. I've never seen a man jump so quickly! Like an ape. Anyone else would have been crushed. Or seriously wounded. He's staggering, but, still has his revolver.

ZAROFF

(Laughs) *Rainsford!* If you are within sound of my voice, as I suppose you are, let me congratulate you. Not many men know how to make a Malay man-catcher. Luckily for me I, too, have hunted in Malacca. You are proving interesting, Mr. Rainsford. I am going now to have my wound dressed... it's only a slight one. But I shall be back. I shall be back.

RAINSFORD

"Gone...the maniac's gone again. Cat and mouse. That's all it is. Well, I have to move on...keep moving. He'll be back in no time. Damn! If he doesn't put an end to me, these insects will!
(MUSIC)

"Well, now...seems I've found the swamp he warned me about. Death Swamp. It sure is. If I go any further, I'll be up to my neck in quicksand. But...that gives me an idea. Start digging... dig, dig, dig....make a pit...cut some branches...sharpen them to a fine point...cover it all up with leaves....gotta move quickly. No time. Arms aching, hands torn and bleeding...can't stop now.
(MUSIC)

"Listen! The soft padding of his feet. It won't be long now, General. I hear you. This way, this way. Ah, the night breeze ...I can even smell your cigarette. What's taking him so long? Come, come...
(CRASH, YELP)

ZAROFF

You've done well, Rainsford! Your Burmese tiger pit has claimed one of my best dogs. Again you score. I think, Mr. Rainsford, I'll see what you can do against my whole pack. I'm going home for a rest now. Thank you for a most amusing evening.
(MUSIC, BIRDS)

RAINSFORD

Well...third day, old boy. You're not going to last, not like this.

Dead tired...starving. Why not? No one said the General is a fair man. Wants a challenge, does he? What kind of a challenge is this? Why don't I just lie here and wait for him and he can put a bullet in me and...

(DISTANT DOG PACK)

"Oh hell! Now, what do I do? I'll never out run those beasts. They're not slow and methodical like the General. They'll be here in no time. Think, boy, think! That's why he's hunting you. Because you've got a mind, you can think...oh Hell...it's a wild chance...but, what else do you have? You've got to move out of the swamp. Climb that tree over the ridge...see what you can see...

(DOGS)

"There he is! Just beyond that field. General Zaroff and...that giant, Ivan. Well, they're all out after me now. They'll be here in minutes. I've got one last trick up my sleeve...learned it in Uganda. When he comes down that path I made ...and he steps on that vine...and that springy sapling comes whipping out with my blade attached to it...bam! But, I can't risk staying around for that. I've got to run. Run like I've never run before. Now I know what an animal feels like when the hunter is at his heels.

(MUSIC, SILENCE, JUNGLE)

"Can't...breathe anymore. Walking up hill. So hot. Weak. Listen...the hounds have stopped. Could it be that the pit has worked? From here I can just see...there's the General...but, I don't see Ivan. Could it be the trap did work...well, somewhat.

(HOUNDS)

"Oh damn! Run you fool...run, even if you have to jump off a cliff. Don't get torn apart by those giant hounds. I won't get eaten by those beasts! I'll jump into the sea before that happens. Then...jump, you fool! Jump from high up here and hope that you'll not hit the rocks below!

(MUSIC)

ZAROFF

So, Rainsford...you have taken the win from me. There will be no trophy tonight. No head to go on my wall. You haven't played fair, my American friend. Now, your body will be smashed against those rocks until there is nothing left. So be it. And, I? I will retire to my home…have an exceedingly good dinner and that bottle of Chateau Lafitte. Of course, I will lament the fact that I no longer have my servant, Ivan. It's going to be very difficult to replace him. Then, I shall spend a relaxing evening in my library.

RAINSFORD
General!

ZAROFF
Rainsford! How in God's name did you get back up here?

RAINSFORD
I never left. Do you see that big rock? I hid like only man can hide…you walked right on by me…so intent you were to look over the cliff's edge to find my body floating in the waves down below.

ZAROFF
I congratulate you. You have won the game.

RAINSFORD
I am still a beast at bay. An animal with its back against the wall. Get ready, General Zaroff.

ZAROFF
Ready?

RAINFORD
Tonight, I shall sleep in *your* bed.

ZAROFF
But, you have no knife…no gun…what do you propose to use to kill me?

RAINFORD
My *teeth*…

ZAROFF
No…no….*no!*

(BLOODY SCREAMS, MUSIC)

Printed in Great Britain
by Amazon.co.uk, Ltd.,
Marston Gate.